"ICE HOCKEY NIGHTS IN EUROPE"

Jonathan Northall

Jonathan Northall

Copyright © 2013 by Jonathan Northall

The right of Jonathan Northall to be identified as author of this work has been asserted by him in accordance with sections 77 and 78 of the Copyright, Designs and Patents Act 1988.

All rights reserved. No part of this publication may be reproduced, stored in retrieval system, copied in any form or by any means, electronic, mechanical, photocopying, recording or otherwise transmitted without written permission from the publisher. You must not circulate this book in any format.

Disclaimer:

NHL is a registered trademark owned by NHL Enterprises, L.P. This book is not affiliated with the National Hockey League (NHL) or any of its teams. Team names, logos, and uniform designs are registered trademarks of the teams displayed.

Ice Hockey Nights in Europe

Jonathan Northall

1 WHO IS YOUR TEAM AND WHY?

It's an obvious question but we have to start at the beginning. As fans, we live so far away from our teams so how come they're our team? For a majority of cases in North America, it was decided before you were born. Perhaps it is the team of your birthplace? Maybe, your parents are staunch fans and it is a "birth right"? For National Hockey League fans outside of the continent, this is less likely. Deciding on a team can be swayed on such a tenuous moment but it will stay forever. This chapter of the book is dedicated to those stories.

My own story is an example of how a random moment or, in my case, item can influence your choice of team. So innocuous a moment it was, I cannot even remember the year but place it around 1992. I somehow came into the possession of a grey t-shirt emblazoned with a large penguin and declaring that the team concerned were 'Prince of Wales Conference champions'. From there, my interest was aroused in the Pittsburgh Penguins and the rest is history. It was at a time before the internet and the world was a larger place than the ever contracting one that it is now. The internet allows us to watch games on our cell (mobile) phones, PC, tablet / iPad, game console etc. My interest in the Penguins would wane over the years but they always seemed to keep finding me. Like many of the stories you will read, the Electronic Arts 'NHL' game series would mean that names like Ulf Samuelsson and Luc Robitaille will be forever linked to the Penguins although they left Pittsburgh a long time ago. The catalyst that caused me to decide that I had to commit fully came in 2008. I had recently started working at an office in Walsall, which is an industrial town in the heart of the West Midlands, and not an ice hockey town at all. One day, I was chatting to a colleague at his desk and just noticed a Penguins logo on his desk. Too much to be a co-incidence, I told myself, I was meant to follow. The colleague was Rob Aherne and you will hear his words later in the book. I thank, and blame, Rob for my late night forays into the world of a European NHL fan.

Greenwich Mean Time (GMT) is 5 hours in front of Eastern Standard Time (EST) and, therefore, 8 hours in front of Pacific Standard Time (PST). This effectively means that a face off at 7pm EST is 12am GMT and 7pm PST is 3am GMT. European fans will only be too well aware of this fact but it helps any North American readers to understand how nocturnal European fans need to be. Added to this, fans from Continental Europe may well be on Central European Time (GMT+1) or worse. Finally, the issue of "Daylight Saving" will have caught many a fan out in the past as they have tuned in only to find the game well underway because North America hasn't switched back from daylight saving yet.

In order to explore the fans stories, I have used the current league structure as a demarcation point. It will be quickly evident that the spread of teams is not even. Personally, I do not think that this is entirely representative of the fan base in Europe and, arguably, just as much my failing to reach fans of those teams.

Eastern Conference

Atlantic Division

New Jersey Devils

My Team is the New Jersey Devils. I started to support them during the 1990's, after getting into hockey playing Mario Lemieux hockey on the Sega Mega Drive, and from my dad telling me about one of his uncles who played hockey in the Navy, I took a interest at quite an early age. When I decided I needed to team to support. Already being a big football (soccer) fan my starting point of searching for a team was team colours, so after narrowing it down I started looking into style of play, not knowing anything about tactics then being young I just liked big hits! So that was what I was looking for a physical team, and New Jersey had Scott Stevens laying people out! And having the great Marty Brodeur in the posts really caught my eye. From then on the Devils had a new fan.

Gavin Clarke
Bristol, England

> Through the years I've followed NHL from afar, watch the odd game but never really had a favourite team until a couple of years ago. The reason I choose the Devils is that I have a few friends in New Jersey who like me have followed The Metrostars / Red Bull New York football (soccer) team. Some of them go regularly to watch the Devils at The Rock.
>
> Orri Smarason
> Reykjavík, Iceland
>
> I don't really know how I got into hockey or even how I became a fan of the Devils but I can only assume that Christmas 2000 must have something to do with it! I received a brand new PlayStation 2 which

Jonathan Northall

came with NHL 2001. I loved that game! In fact, I still have it. I played that game for months on end. Why did I choose the New Jersey Devils? Again, I'm not 100% sure. I think it was because when I was 9 or 10, my parents took me to Philadelphia to visit a friend of my father. Now, you'd think that he would be a Flyers fan but he was most definitely a Devils fan! I think this had a huge influence on me! Between the age of 11 and 18 I seemed to lose my connection with hockey but at 18 I began to watch the Devils almost religiously. As a 'fresher' at university, I stayed up for EVERY game in the 2009/2010 season. As I live in the UK, this meant that most games started at 12am GMT.

Andreas Tatt
Bristol, England

I always liked ice hockey but until I was about 15 or 16 I only followed the Italian Championship. Following the Devils started with soccer and my father's passion for AC Milan (Milan colours are red and black and are called "the Devils") In 1989, Milan sports club bought Milano hockey team renaming it Devils Milano (of course, their colours were red and black) and it was quite natural I become their fan. It was then that my "summer" friends told me of the NHL team called New Jersey Devils: same name, same colours, how I couldn't become a fan?

Emanuela Pozzi
Cernusco sul Naviglio, Italy

New York Islanders

My team is the New York Islanders simply because a few of my friends support the Rangers and I wanted to support a "less popular" team!!!

James Cartwright
Cardiff, Wales

Islanders. Why? I live in Warsaw, Poland - the same city where Marre Czerkawski lives now. He was first reason to support New York Islanders. When Isles traded Marre, my heart stayed in Long Island because I love New York! This is the city where I would live. Since 2003 when I could connected by Internet at home, I support my Isles. Every night, when Islanders play, I spent time listening to the radio (a few years ago) then NHL GameCenter. A last few years wasn't good for Isles fans, for me too.

Ice Hockey Nights in Europe

But I'm loyal and faithful. I wonder whether the bad times are the past now and good players like John Tavares, Travis Hamonic or Josh Bailey are glimmers of hope.

Mikołaj Wójcik
Warsaw, Poland

<u>New York Rangers</u>

Ironically for me, it wasn't actually hockey that led me to the Rangers. I had always loved New York City, or at least the idea of it. Small kid, big city; it was somewhere that I had always dreamed of visiting from a young age. I kind of took a partial interest in hockey, as best as I could anyway, and chose the Rangers due to the NYC connection and the fact they were an Original Six team. But it was only after visiting New York and going to a Rangers/Penguins game (which the Rangers won in a shootout) at Madison Square Garden that my interest in hockey - and, more specifically, the Rangers - really picked up. Naturally the Rangers became and stayed 'my' team, and despite their fair share of disappointments post-lockout, I'm proud to call them mine. Proud of their work ethic, their determination and, of course, the largely home-grown, drafted roster. So, thanks New York City, I owe you one!

Alex Nunn
Romford, England

My NHL team is New York Rangers. My "fan career" started in 2008, when my parents visited in NYC. They saw one Rangers game and after that I was hooked on Rangers. In the first season, I watched couple of games on TV. After that we bought NHL GameCenter Live and we watched every game. In that time we woke up at 2am to catch up the games. In 2010, we visited New York and I saw couple of games at Madison Square Garden. We had tickets to two games but on the spot we bought tickets to Rangers last home game of the regular-season (kind of expensive one at $195 each).

Ville Lampinen
Vantaa, Finland

The reason I am a fan of the NY Rangers is because we were on a school trip to New York and part of the trip was a chance to go and watch an ice hockey game between the Rangers and Florida Panthers. We went to the game and I started to take everything in. The atmosphere of MSG, the fans and most importantly the game! It wasn't a great game, the team lost 4-2 and didn't play well, but the seeds had been planted. I was interested. When I got back home, I started to follow the team casually, check on their results and after a while, I started to watch it and that is how I got into the game. Now I'm hooked!

Daruish Gorgirzadeh
Bournemouth, England

I live in Somerset in the south west of England but the New York Rangers are my team. I used to play NHL games on my Playstation when I was younger and I always watched it in the Olympics, however I never really gave the league a chance. My brother-in-law went to watch the Edmonton Oilers play whilst on holiday and he was telling me how good the sport was. I gave it a go on ESPN and thought 'wow, this is good'. I knew to fully enjoy it I would need to a team to follow. As a massive fan of the NFL and in particular the New York Giants, it was a natural move to follow the Rangers. Both teams were established organisations, not some upstart new team and both had been relatively starved of success so there could be no bandwagon jumping claims. Also, it's not out of the question that I would be able to watch a game, should we holiday to New York.

Ed Johnston
Somerset, England

Philadelphia Flyers

My team is the Philadelphia Flyers for the simple reason that I was born thirty miles from Philadelphia and spent the first seven years of my life in the area. My dad shared a season ticket with one of his work colleagues, and either he or my mum used to take me to the afternoon games. As a result, I've been a Flyers fan for as long as I remember.

Tim Barnes
Cambridge, England

My team was chosen all down to a core of 5 players that I admired greatly: Mark Recchi, John LeClair, Eric Lindros, Mikael Renberg and Eric Desjardins. They played a huge part in why I follow the Philadelphia Flyers. A late cousin of mine (whose parents were chasing down their family roots; as was my father at the time) flew in from Chicago, circa 1997, and he was a Blackhawks fan and I can remember him raving about the United Centre crowd on game-days. Jonathan, my cousin, taught me the basic rules of hockey and tried to persuade me to become a Chi-town fan. I was adamant in waiting to watch a little bit of hockey before deciding which team to support. It was not until I found NHL highlights on one of our only 4 channels at the time.

David Lidbury
Bristol, England

So how does a small town boy become a fan of Hockey team based thousands of miles away? The question should not be how did I become a fan, more, because of whom, did I become a fan? The answer is Jack Patterson. In my early teens, I, along with my parents and 2 younger siblings were lucky enough to visit distant (in both senses of the word) relatives in Canada, one of these relatives was Jack. Jack was a big man, and an even bigger Hockey fan, he was also active within his local hockey community, both his sons played the game. Now I was lucky enough to go and see the local WHL team (The Kamloops Blazers) with Jack. This was the first time I'd been to a hockey game, and I was hooked. After playing hockey on his driveway one evening, Jack showed us round his family home. His sons had jerseys, banners, pennants and every other item of merchandise you could imagine... the colours? Orange and Black!! I can still vividly recall seeing an Eric Lindros Jersey hanging in one of the rooms. Jack sadly passed away on the 13th April 2004. I owe Jack a lot: he took me to my first hockey game, gave me a hockey stick (that I still have), and a puck that I hold while watching the Flyers play, I have no idea why, other than it makes me feel like he is watching with me. My passion for the Philadelphia Flyers is down to him. RIP Jack.

Benn Mixer
Stalham, England

I became a fan of the Flyers thanks to a school exchange trip to Doylestown, PA back in 2007. The Flyers seemed to be constantly on the local television there and I really enjoyed the Flyers highlights due to the skill and physicality of the team. Once I returned home they became my team.

Ray Skeates
Basingstoke, England

So how does a small town boy become a fan of Hockey team based thousands of miles away? The question should not be how did I become a

fan, more, because of whom, did I become a fan? The answer is Jack Patterson. In my early teens, I, along with my parents and 2 younger siblings were lucky enough to visit distant (in both senses of the word) relatives in Canada, one of these relatives was Jack. Jack was a big man, and an even bigger Hockey fan, he was also active within his local hockey community, both his sons played the game. Now I was lucky enough to go and see the local WHL team (The Kamloops Blazers) with Jack. This was the first time I'd been to a hockey game, and I was hooked. After playing hockey on his driveway one evening, Jack showed us round his family home. His sons had jerseys, banners, pennants and every other item of merchandise you could imagine... the colours? Orange and Black!! I can still vividly recall seeing an Eric Lindros Jersey hanging in one of the rooms. Jack sadly passed away on the 13th April 2004. I owe Jack a lot: he took me to my first hockey game, gave me a hockey stick (that I still have), and a puck that I hold while watching the Flyers play, I have no idea why, other than it makes me feel like he is watching with me. My passion for the Philadelphia Flyers is down to him.
RIP Jack.

Benn Mixer
Stalham, England

Pittsburgh Penguins

Perhaps this is a strange way of picking which team you'll support at a sport but I became a Penguins fan after playing NHL 98. I kept randomising the team selection until I stopped at the Pittsburgh Penguins.
What made me stop at the Pens? Penguins were my favourite animal! I kept playing as them on the computer games and it stuck and I became a fan!

James Bird
Burnley, England

I actually attended my first hockey game back in 1992 when they first started playing pro hockey in Sheffield (England). I didn't go to a game until the 1999/00 season when my then new girlfriend, and who's now my wife, invited me to a Sheffield Steelers game – her family were all season ticket holders. Begrudgingly I went along. Fast forward 12 months to Christmas 2000 and we went away for a romantic few days in York. On our way home from the theatre, I bought a copy of "Face-Off" magazine from a shop. In the magazine was an article about this NHL team called the Pittsburgh Penguins. The article described how the team was currently

Ice Hockey Nights in Europe

struggling and how their former star player – a guy called Mario Lemieux – now owned the team. When we got back to our hotel I happened to flick through the TV listings and noticed that there was an NHL game being shown recorded from the previous night. The date was December 28th 2000. So much to my girlfriend's annoyance, I sat up to watch the game. Needless to say from that moment on I was a Pens' fan. My home town of Sheffield is, of course, twinned with Pittsburgh. They are both steel towns, built on hills with major rivers running through them. And of course the original Stanley Cup was made in Sheffield! The Pens have now become a massive part of my life. Amongst the many things I could say, I covered the Pens for the website InsideHockey.com for a couple of years, I now own six Pens' jerseys, before he was 2 years old my eldest son could recognise (and say) both the Pens logo and the Stanley Cup, my youngest son has 'Crosby' as his second middle name (I wasn't allowed 'Mario' or 'Lemieux' for my eldest son). I am immensely proud that a picture of the four of us in Pens' jerseys is part of the Mario Mosaic.

One day, we will return to Pittsburgh and get to see our photo in person.

Rob Howe
Sheffield, England

My favourite team are the Pittsburgh Penguins. The love affair started when I was about 6. That was the first time someone told me that there are other leagues than our local league of 8 teams. When I came home, I asked my Dad, which is the best hockey league in the world? Obviously he said NHL. I asked him about the teams and he started naming all 30 of them. I remembered only Penguins, since penguins were my favourite animals at the time.

Sanja Prošek
Ljubljana, Slovenia

I was 6½ when I saw my first live hockey game. My first live NHL game - December 31st, 1988. The date of this game will forever be remembered by hockey historians. Whereas I will always remember the date because on this day I fell in love with Mario Lemieux, the Pittsburgh Penguins and the NHL. And as it turned out, I happened to witness one of the finest individual scoring performances ever in the NHL.

Mario scored a hat trick in the first period, and went on to score a goal in every possible way in the pre-shootout era (even strength, shorthanded, powerplay, penalty shot, and empty net).

There is no way I would ever be able to support another team after this experience, and it will always remain one of my fondest memories. I have been an avid Penguins fan ever since....

Stephen Butler
Leicester, England

Northeast Division

<u>Boston Bruins</u>

As a family, we went to a Guildford Flames hockey game at the beginning of the 2010/11 season. We just loved the game and so kept on going. This led us to buying a subscription to ESPN and watching the NHL games. We started watching all different teams and then we watched a Boston game. The game was brilliant and it went to penalties. Tim Thomas was amazing in goal, he never gave up on a puck. I then looked up his story and then the rest of the teams. Since that game we never looked back and have been fans of the Bruins ever since.

Amy Hill
Camberley, England

I am a hockey newbie. My friend took me to my first game, last February. I had never watched hockey before in my entire life, and knew nothing about it. However, I am not exactly a sports fan, so I took a book just in case I got bored! Anyway, once our season finished, I felt withdrawal symptoms and started to research into the NHL. The first games I watched were the playoff run between Boston and the Habs (Montreal Canadiens). One of my greatest hockey moments so far, has to be when Timmy Thomas just dropped Hank Sedin. As well as staying up until 6am to see Chara look like all his Christmases had come at once when he finally got to hoist the cup. Timmy pretty much weeping when he got the Conn Smythe on top of the cup. I would absolutely love to go to Boston during playoff season to sit in TD Garden, and soak up the NHL atmosphere.

Kimmi Noble
Sheffield, England

I am a relatively new convert to Ice Hockey with main passion beginning around February 2011. I tried to watch as many games as I could late at night on ESPN America and I was immediately drawn to the Bruins; They were a hard-hitting, tough and determined team balanced both defensively and offensively which appealed straight away. What drew me in was their rich history of Orr, Esposito, Bourque, Sanderson, Neely, Bucyk; gritty talented players! I've never been to Boston or even USA/Canada, but Bruins were MY team. The name and colours itself resonated with my local Hockey team with the B's, (Bracknell Bees) and it seemed a natural fit to support the Bruins. Little did I know that as soon as I begin to follow them, they complete a successful Stanley Cup run, since then I've been trying to avoid being a bandwagon fan but I feel I can stick with them through thick and thin whatever happens now!

Andrew Best
Bracknell, England

I met a former Bruins captain and their current assistant coach Doug Houda, at a gig I was playing. They very kindly gave me free tickets to the Bruins v Giants game happening the next night. Little did I know what impact the game was going to have on my life! My friend and I had centre ice seats right in front of the Bruins bench, and I spent the whole game transfixed by the action, even though I had no idea what was happening. I just knew that the sport I was watching was different, and the players were different and the atmosphere in the arena was different to any sporting event I had been to before. I remember watching team Captain Zdeno Chara, and thinking he was the most amazing thing I'd ever seen, I had no idea he was the tallest player in the league, I was just impressed with his poise with the puck, the area he could create for himself on the ice and the way he seemed to be the glue that held everything together. I might not have understood the rules of the game but I could see that the Bruins had some special quality to them right away. I guess the reason why I find my team so irreplaceable, is because their passion for the game is always present. It's there when they win, when each line is overachieving and scoring with panache and that trademark Bruins swagger appears.

Eilis Phillips
Belfast, Northern Ireland

Buffalo Sabres

My team are the Buffalo Sabres. I don't really remember why they became the team I followed when I started watching the NHL in 2008. Maybe it was because they had a well-known German player in Jochen Hecht and two German prospects. A bunch of other teams also had Germans and I never really followed them. Now, a few years after I started watching NHL and after some disappointing seasons for the Sabres, I've often asked myself the same question that was asked.

David Trippler
Mainz, Germany

I started off with hockey through games. Not playing actual ice hockey. That was difficult as I lived in the United Arab Emirates as a kid so there was very little chance to ever play. No, NHL 94 and NHL 96. I didn't really have a team, I just picked whoever at that time. Later on, when my brothers got into it, I saw the new Buffalo Sabres jersey. My favourite colours were Black and Red, the crest of the charging Buffalo was cool and then the icing on the cake was Miroslav Satan. Any heavy metal fan would find a guy whose last name was Satan to be pretty cool. I didn't pay too much attention back then. We got very few games if any on TV while I lived in the UAE and even less when I first moved back to the UK. In 2008 I started to pay more attention because my younger brother (who was a diehard Avalanche fan) told me we the Sabres doing quite well. We were, it was the start of the season, we were #1 in the league and Thomas Vanek was the top goal scorer. Unfortunately we missed the playoffs in the end but after watching the 2009 Stanley Cup playoffs I was hooked. After every game that's all I could think about.

David Robertson
Aberdeen, Scotland

Montreal Canadiens

I grew up with hockey being a big part of my life. When I was younger, my team was Edmonton Oilers because I idolised Jari Kurri. However, I became a Montreal Canadiens fan later on in life for many reasons to be honest. I had followed the career of Saku Koivu in Finland and where his team - TPS - dominated the league back in those days, I always saw something in Koivu, partially due to the 1995 World Championships and the line he formed with Jere Lehtinen and Ville Peltonen. When Koivu left for the NHL, I started following the Habs and the more I followed the team the more my interest grew in the history of the team. When I explored the history of the Canadiens they were, to me, the most prolific team to have played the game. They hold the most Stanley Cups and have had many of the games' brightest stars and legends play for them, from Maurice and Henri Richard, Georges Vezina, 'Boom Boom' Geofrion (the inventor of the slapshot) and so on. The list is literally endless. The Canadiens, or Habs, are a team that exudes winning and, in many ways, the Canadiens "CH" logo has become synonymous with winning, just as the Winged Wheel of the Detroit jersey. Even though I criticize the Habs nowadays and give a lot of flack to one Scott Gomez, I still remain a fan and supporter of the team. Not just one player but the team. I've had the fortune of having French Canadian team mates during my hockey career who have shared my affinity with the Habs and I have been able to recount the triumphs and the low points of their seasons.

Janne Virtanen
Hameenlinna, Finland (now Basingstoke, England)

Love the jersey and the fans stay loyal to the team. The main reason I like them though is their history. They are the oldest team in the NHL and had some of the best players ever in the NHL. e.g. Roy, Richard, Lafleur. They were the last Canadian team to win the Stanley Cup . I have followed hockey for a while but Montreal's playoff run a few years ago is what really got me behind them. I liked the way they play and the fact that they were the underdogs that season looking to win their 25th cup. I have been a Habs fan ever since and stay up at night to watch them even with college the next morning, hoping for a win and a chance in the playoffs. Everyone has a dream for their team to win the Cup which is why they support them. I support Montreal because of the French pride, their never say die attitude and the unrivalled atmosphere that is generated by their fans.

Diarmuid Murray
Dublin, Rep of Ireland

Although I now live in Scotland, I am Canadian and grew up watching Hockey Night in Canada. Every Saturday night, with the snow lying on the ground outside and the fire roaring inside, we would turn on the TV to watch the game. Living in Ontario, the team we usually saw was the Leafs and most of my friends and family are Leafs fans. But sometimes, we got to see the Canadiens and in the 1970s & 1980s, they had one of the most graceful, talented, skillful, popular player on their roster. That was Guy LaFleur - he was amazing to watch and he made me a Canadiens fan.

Sharon Wedley
North Ayrshire, Scotland

My team, by sheer good fortune, happens to be the most successful franchise in hockey history in terms of Stanley Cup wins, Le Canadien de

Jonathan Northall

Montreal. I'd imagine my new found passion and fandom for this team was launched in the same way as countless others from the UK, by chance whilst on holiday. In my case, I had been travelling in May 2010 throughout Eastern Canada, and ended up in Montreal just as the Canadiens were in the midst of an epic playoff run which had gripped the city. I had no real knowledge of NHL upon arriving in the city, but it become immediately apparent that something big was happening upon my arrival. The Canadiens logo and merchandise was everywhere: on shop windows, buses, cars and so on. On my second evening whilst there, the Habs as they are known were playing at home in the Bell Centre against Pittsburgh Penguins in Game Six. My fiancé and I decided to get into the spirit and ventured downtown to firstly mill around the arena to take in the atmosphere and to find a pub to settle in to watch the game. The Habs won the game to tie the series and take it to a 'winner takes all' game a few nights later. Watching the game in a Montreal watering hole was thoroughly exciting and we certainly got a sample of the Quebecois passion for their team as final hooter went and thousands of people took to the streets to celebrate. I am now a fully fledged fan and have travelled throughout North America on numerous occasions to follow the team. Long may it continue!

Chris Roderick
Ammanford, Wales

Ottawa Senators

Ottawa Senators are my team. I chose them over a decade ago while playing EA Sports NHL. This game wasn't enough for me, I started to follow up Senators. I chose them because of few reasons. First of all - they are Canadian team. I always liked this country so it was a natural choice for me. Secondly, in Ottawa played a lot of players from Europe, especially from Sweden: Daniel Alfredsson (today my favourite player), Andreas Dackel, Magnus Arvedson and others: Radek Bonk, Marian Hossa, Sami Salo, Alexei Yashin etc. Senators are my team since 2000. And will be forever.

Krzysztof Sankiewicz
Warsaw, Poland

My team is the Ottawa Senators, three of years ago hockey was something I only experienced in video games and had little knowledge or understanding of, but that all changed in 2010. Watching ice hockey in the Vancouver Winter Olympics, seeing Crosby score and Canada win gold gave me a taste of the fast paced action and excitement of watching NHL games. After watching the odd game here and there I needed a team to support and I chose the Ottawa Senators. The main reason I chose them was that a friend of mine from work watches hockey, he was born in Canada near Ottawa and he supports the Sens so it seemed like a good enough reason to start following the team. After watching a few games and seeing big players like Daniel Alfredsson, Jason Spezza and young stars like Erik Karlsson play I was hooked. Hockey is now by far my favourite sport to watch and I regularly stay up late to catch as many of Ottawa's game as I can.

Robert Weaver
Gloucestershire, England

So, my favourite NHL team is Ottawa Senators, because Latvian guy Kaspars Daugavins plays there.

Elina Lazdina
Talsi, Latvia

Toronto Maple Leafs

Whilst on my first vacation to Toronto, a friend took me to the ACC to watch the Toronto Maple Leafs play the St Louis Blues. Not knowing much about ice hockey, except its reputation for fighting, I really didn't know what to expect. I was blown away by the speed and hitting on the ice. Although struggling to catch onto most of the rules as a novice, I really enjoyed the game and the atmosphere was great as the Leafs stretched out into a 5-0 lead. As much as to make sure I was ready for future disappointment, the Leafs allowed the game to be tied at 5-5 before losing the game in overtime. Despite the heart breaking loss I was hooked for life with my new sporting heroes being Domi, Sundin & Cujo.

Mark Rackham
Kent, England

For me it's the Toronto Maple Leafs, it was always going to be the Leafs, but it's difficult to say exactly why. It could well be in part to "50 Mission Cap" by The Tragically Hip, it could be because they are the most famous brand in hockey. Most likely though it's because in November 2007 I visited Canada for the first time, I fell in love with the city of Toronto. On my last day before heading home some friends took my wife (though at that point we were not yet married) and I to Niagara for the day. In the evening, we went to an Irish pub somewhere in the suburbs sadly I cannot remember it's name. What I do remember though is eating some great steak, drinking Guinness and watching Hockey Night in Canada. From then on, I tried to keep in touch with the Leafs goings on.

Matt Merritt
Portsmouth, England

Having been born in Ireland, I moved to Canada when just a child and I spent my early childhood living in southern Ontario and was hooked. Living where I did, there was no escaping the Leafs as they were always on TV and all the other kids were Leafs fans too! Having moved back to Ireland, and subsequently been living back here for the last 18 years, I have continued to follow them through thick and thin (mostly thin) and still have that same blind passion for my team as I did as kid growing up!

Christopher Barr
Dungannon, Northern Ireland

I have been a hockey fan since the mid-90s, started with my home team, Manchester Storm. I properly starting following the Leafs team around 1998-99 season. I have relatives in Canada, and many are in Toronto, so I have spend many a holiday over there. It is slowly becoming a second home to me. I saw a game on the TV and became fascinated with the it all. It just seemed natural to me to be a Leafs fan. I haven't looked back since.

Rachael Eardley
Manchester, England

Southeast Division

Carolina Hurricanes

My team is the Carolina Hurricanes. In all honesty, it was a bit of a random decision! My friends and I all got into going to see our local team, the Nottingham Panthers, when we were about 16. The game really took a hold on me, the quickness of it, the noise and atmosphere in the arena, it was all great! I eventually decided to get a game for my PS2 so I could enjoy it away from the arena too. NHL 2K7 was the first game I bought, and I had to decide on a team to use since obviously there wasn't any British Elite League teams. I wanted a bit of challenge, I didn't want to choose the best statistical team nor the worse, so I went with one of the middling upper teams and decided upon the Canes. I liked the look of their jerseys and thought their name was pretty cool too! I began to roughly follow them online too and was pleasantly surprised to discover that they were the defending Stanley Cup champs. So I "followed" them very roughly until I went to university in Lincoln in 2007. Being away from the home arena of the Nottingham Panthers made it a bit more difficult to keep up with them because although they have a website it is not as frequently updated with news so I began to follow the Canes a lot more closely. I would check the various news websites several times a day, and even more when I was procrastinating and trying to avoid doing work! By this time too I had also got an Xbox 360 and many, many hours were spent with university friends playing the various NHL games (I have bought every yearly title since that first one I got, and defected to the EA series in time for the NHL09 game). Even being back in Nottingham now I would say I still follow the Canes more closely than I do the Panthers.

I would probably describe myself as a digital fan, obviously I don't get to see many games.

Adam Webster
Nottingham, England

I've always thought I would enjoy hockey but not having access to it on TV made it difficult to get into properly, until getting with my current boyfriend who bought the online pass. I support them because of my family ties to NC, I've spent a lot of time out there so feel a connection to the state. Plus they live only about an hour drive from Raleigh so I feel pretty close to the team's base.

Kelly Marriot
Bournemouth, England

Florida Panthers

My love of ice hockey started in 2001 when I was 11yrs old. I was in town with my mum one day and went into a CD shop to have a look around. I went to see which Playstation 1 games they had, and I saw a copy of NHL 2000. My mum told me that I probably wouldn't like it but bought it anyway. As soon as I got home I put it on and I had to decide which team to play as. I thought about the Penguins and the Sharks but since I was going to Florida a few weeks later, I should go for the Panthers. Whilst in Florida, my mum bought me my first Panthers jersey at Universal. That was me, an official fan! 11yrs later I still own that same jersey plus another 5 and

Jonathan Northall

I have stuck with them through both good and bad times.

Aimee Docherty
Port Glasgow, Scotland

My favourite team is the Florida Panthers and has been for the last 16 years. When I was a young kid my dad worked with the stepdad of Johan Garpenlöv, a then Panther, and my dad got some autographed hockey cards of Garpenlöv. Being a young kid, even if Garpenlöv wasn't really a star, was amazing and a highlight of my life in general. As it has gone on longer and longer, the team have struggled and I keep thinking back to the '96 series and realize how good the team performed. Watching highlights of the playoff series where John "Beezer" Vanbiesbrouck stole game after game and really performed so good that he, as the only NHL goaltender yet and the first ever player to be on the cover of a NHL-game, earned the honour to be the cover guy for the game.

Dan Edlund
Stockholm, Sweden

It all started in around 1996 we retuned our TV so we could get the NHL games on Channel 5. I picked and followed Florida Panthers and went to Tampa Bay, buying a Panthers jersey, and walked around getting weird looks in Tampa. I liked the way they played and, of course, they have the coolest jerseys though they were hardly ever on TV. Now I have no choice but to watch online and cheer at my netbook and laptop.

Rebecca Hindle
Manchester, England

Tampa Bay Lightning

We are hockey fans for years, following the NHL especially to see all the European players. Additionally, we are attending a few hockey games every year here in Germany. However, we could not attend as much as we want because our favorite German team are "Eisbaeren" which are located 500 miles away from our home in South Germany. After not visiting the United States for a few years after the birth of our son, we choose to spend our holidays in Florida because of the children related attractions. So, 2008 was our first time to visit Florida and we choose to attend a game between the Lightning and the Panthers at the Forum in Tampa. It was an exciting experience to see "Hockey under Palms". Half a year later we spent time in

Ice Hockey Nights in Europe

Switzerland to attend games at the IIHF World Championships and saw a game featuring Canada. The two best players were Martin St. Louis and Steven Stamkos. Since then, we spent our holidays every autumn in the Tampa Bay area and visited some Lightning games.

Alexander, Daniela & Marek Neumann
Schwäbisch Hall, Germany

I've been a hockey fan since 1998 but didn't follow the NHL until the 2001-02 season. I wasn't always as avid fan as I am now and only since 2003 I've had a team I would truly love. It was the end of the 2002-03 season when my father, who likes to travel and one of his favorite destinations is Florida, brought a gift for me from Tampa. It was a Tampa Bay Lightning cap and that's how it all started for me. I figured that now that I have their hat I might as well want follow the Lightning a bit more. Year after year my love for them kept growing and now they're my number one love in the NHL, if not the whole hockey world.

Katerina Brzonova
Zlin, Czech Republic

I'm originally from Bristol, England but moved to Tampa, From that, as you can guess, my Team is the Tampa Bay Lightning. I started to follow the Lightning in 2002, I attended my first game while on holiday in Sarasota with my parents. After being obsessed with the Mighty Ducks films as a kid, my dad had always said if we ever made it to America on holiday, we would try and see a game. When my parents booked to go to Florida, I was excited to see that there was an NHL team around 45 minutes away. I then bought the latest NHL computer game and started to play as the Bolts to learn all the players names, and this guy on the game seemed pretty good, his name was Vincent Lecavalier. On holiday, we contacted the Lightning and booked the tickets, and the game against the Bruins was packed, I was instantly hooked. The Lightning won the game 5-2 and I went away a fan for life! I continued to follow the team via the web and Channel 5 in the UK, broadcasting games once a week. The next season, the Lightning won the Stanley Cup and I was up every night until 4/5am watching every minute, even with school the next day. I've been a fan since that first game and made many trips back across the pond to watch my Bolts. On one of those I met my now wife! And I now live the dream of being a Lightning season ticket holder!

Nathan Cartmel
Bristol, England (now Tampa, FL, USA)

Jonathan Northall

I grew up in Rimouski, Quebec, and watched Vincent Lecavalier and Brad Richards through their junior season while supporting my local team. My friends through university each had their team to which they were loyal, and when I finally decided to join the club, I chose Tampa Bay to support Vincent and Brad. They then won me over with their fast pace style and won the Stanley Cup two years after.

Youri Banville
Rimouski, Canada (now Shrivenham, UK)

<u>Washington Capitals</u>

It is the Capitals because they're the first team I started watching. I've always gone to watch my local hockey team since the age of 5 but at that age and growing up I had no way of watching the NHL. It was only when I got older and started watching clips on YouTube of Alex Ovechkin that I started watching his games to see how he was getting on and wanting him to do well which just led to me wanting the team to do well.

Hana Imiolczyk
Merthyr Tydfil, Wales

Not really sure why. I started watching NHL in the UK and saw a Caps game. Ovi was up to his usual high standard of play and I kind of fell for the team. I followed the Redskins in the NFL so it made sense to stick with a city I knew a little about. Since my love for the Caps, I have travelled to DC and watched a game live from the arena. For those other fans I also drove to Pittsburgh so my daughter could watch the Penguins play the following night, I even saw Crosby get a hat-trick that night, still it's the 'reds' for me.

Nick Gresty
Manchester, England

<u>Winnepeg Jets</u>

It all started with Ondřej Pavelec because he's Czech. Then, Pavelec went as a number one goalie for the Czech national team at the World Championships 2011 and he's quickly become my favorite goalie. Now, of course, I love the whole team. Every one of them, unconditionally, but Pav remains my favourite. When they moved I felt sorry for the Atlanta fans, but since I'm from the other end of the world, I didn't really mind, after all it's still the same team. So I "moved" with them. And I think that was a great move. Winnipeg fans are just the best, they are loyal, loud and supportive. One of the many things I hate about living so far is that I have to get up at 1am or 3am, whenever the game is, but it's definitely worth it every time. My biggest dream right now is going to Winnipeg for one whole hockey season and going to every home game.

Štěpánka Černá
Dolní Němčí, Czech Republic

Western Conference

Central Division

Chicago Blackhawks

I initially followed the Chicago Bears in 1984....I was seven years old. I had Illinois based pen friends, an older couple by the name of Audley and Fern Risley. I can remember some gifts they sent over being wrapped in a local sports paper...and a small piece written on the Blackhawks. It wasn't until the arrival of Sky TV and Eurosport that I got to see them for the first time at a family friends BBQ in the early 1990's.

Nathan Hollis
Norwich, England

I remember listening to American Forces Network, under the blankets, with a torch on a very small transistor rather a lot of years ago in Wales. For me, it was the name that got me hooked was "Blackhawks"! One of my favourite comics, at that time, also featured the 'BlackHawks'. Lost a bit of interest as I was getting older until I arrived in London and got talked into going to Streatham to see the Redskins and I was hooked all over again. It rekindled my interest in the Hawks and as I had a friend who worked at one of the top London hotels he use to bring me the Sport pages from any US paper he found. I think Hossa is fantastic and Savard was a great player. Also, our keeper Antti Niemi when we won the cup was outstanding.

Steve Robinson
London, England

I got interested in hockey during the Winter Olympics in 2010 and this little dude named Patrick Kane really caught my eye. After a couple of weeks, I noticed it started bothering me during my schooldays if I didn't know how last night's Hawks game had ended. That is when I started considering myself as a fan. It took me a while to figure some terms out and get some kind of base to my hockey knowledge, but I am proud I did it, and all by myself too. Being an NHL fan in Europe is something people who don't watch any hockey admire or think is extremely stupid. Even though Finland is a country where everyone loves hockey, some men still seem to think it's impossible for women to understand hockey. There's been a couple of situations where I've had to prove I understand hockey, like explain what an icing is or name the last three Stanley Cup champions and their captains etc. It is a little frustrating, but I'll never get used to seeing a man's face when I first let him know I understand hockey and possibly can prove him wrong about something.

Satu Vanhanen
Joensuu, Finland

My team is the Chicago Blackhawks. The reason being, when I first got into ice hockey I downloaded the demo of the game "NHL 11". There were only 2 teams to available to play as, one of which was the Blackhawks. I chose them and through playing the game, began to know the players and their information. So when I finally got round to watching the NHL, it seemed an obvious choice to support Chicago seeing as I knew more about them than any other team. One year on, and my passion for the Hawks has only got stronger!

Darren Morgan
Glasgow, Scotland

Columbus Blue Jackets

Despite currently being the worst team in the league, and arguably the most unfashionable, I support the Columbus Blue Jackets. The primary reason for subjecting myself to this ordeal is that I have family who have lived in the city since the 1980s and when I became a fan of ice hockey from watching late-night broadcasts of the NHL during my student days, there was no other team for me. Even if I did not have these family ties, there are number of reasons that the Blue Jackets would appeal to me. Firstly, they are a young club formed only in 2000, meaning that I don't have to trawl through decades of history to understand them and also ensures that I will be able to experience any success that they achieve while I am a fan. It would perhaps be slightly unoriginal to pick one of the traditionally more successful or more high profile teams. I am proud to be a Blue Jackets fan and enjoy people's bemused reactions when I tell them which club I support.

Steve McCaskill
Maidstone, England

Detroit Red Wings

Being a fan of the (NFL's Green Bay) Packers who have a loyal fan base whether they are losing or winning and do things the right way, I wanted my NHL team to reflect that. After looking at the different teams and reading information about them, I decided to pick the Red Wings. They are a model franchise in the NHL that any fan could be proud of. They have sellout crowds, not sign big Free Agents but rather draft and develop their own guys, and are pillar of the community on and off the field.

Junaid Hussain
Nottingham, England

It started with NHLPA '93 on the Sega Mega Drive (Genesis) and I just fell in love with them from the start. It was Steve Yzerman that really drew me to the team, well, his little pixelised avatar anyhow. I may be called a glory hunter I suppose, as I was young and they were likely the best team on the game, but I made sure over the years I knew everything about the history of the franchise. Despite being born across the Atlantic, this team will hold a special place in my heart.

Bradley Marsh
Essex, England

My team of choice is the Detroit Red Wings. They were playing a game against Boston, so I decided to record it overnight and watch it the morning after. As soon as I started watching, I fell in love with the team, and everything about them. The way they play the game stood out to me from other teams in the league, as did the fans in the arena, the jerseys, and the announcers. Since then I've loved the team, and will continue to do so, I honestly feel that I didn't find the team, the team found me.

Joe Alderson
Stoke-on-Trent, England

Jonathan Northall

My team are the Detroit Red Wings. My unhealthy obsession dates back to 1994, and a Sega Mega Drive. I'd wanted to buy Urban Strike, a game about attack helicopters, but I didn't have enough money. I did have enough, however, for NHL '94. This started an obsession of playing with multiple teams, and players whose names soon became as familiar as the top footballers of the day. What made it a little more special, was that nobody I knew had even heard of the NHL, so the sport was 'mine' as it were. It became worse when I started to watch late night Channel 5 (TV) games. I'd enjoyed playing NHL '94 with the Red Wings, as I found Fedorov and Yzerman most suited to my playing desires, but when I saw the team play on TV, it was someone else who caught my eye. Enter Bob Probert. A guy who played like the fans wanted to play, he pushed himself to the limit every shift, gave everything he possibly could, and scared the living daylights out of opposition players. Nearly 20 years later, I've been to Detroit to see the team play in the Joe Louis Arena. I grow a playoff beard every post-season, and I lose weeks of sleep staying up to watch the games live. I wouldn't change a single thing.

Stuart Wilson
York, England

Nashville Predators

I've been a hockey fan since 2003-2004 season. I was 13 at the time. My friend from school, a Mighty Ducks of Anaheim fan, told me to listen/watch a few games, and that's how the story started. I remember watching games involving the Senators, Devils, Ducks and a few more teams. Also, I tested some teams whilst playing the EA Sports video game. The search for my favourite team ended when I watched a game between the Detroit Red Wings and the Nashville Predators. I just loved how hard working, low-profile, under the radar the Preds were. I probably didn't even know where Nashville was on the map. I immediately fell in love with Scott Walker who became my first favourite player. Then came the Steve Sullivan transfer and his debut in Preds uniform, in which he scored hat-trick on just three shots, leading the Preds to a 7-3 win over the San Jose Sharks. Since then, it's just been Predators all the way! From the first visit to the playoffs, through the firesale in 2007, up to now.

Paweł Jachowski
Siedlce, Poland

Ice Hockey Nights in Europe

St Louis Blues

I discovered the Blues about 7 years ago after being badgered by a US friend of mine to actually watch a game of hockey. My friend, Pam, is from Orange County, California and supports the Los Angeles Kings. She's a hockey goalie. After a few months of her constantly talking about hockey, I finally succumbed and decided to watch a game. In the UK at that time, only one television channel showed hockey games – one game a week in the early hours of Thursday mornings. I took a day off work, stayed up and watched a game. The game was the St Louis Blues versus the Detroit Red Wings. Shortly after the puck dropped, I was hooked. The game was fast and physical – not at all what I was expecting. The Red Wings won the game but the Blues were the team that impressed me. It was obvious that the Red Wings had the talent but the Blues were the workers...and they never stopped...never gave up. I loved their attitude. A couple of weeks later, I watched another game, a game between two Eastern Conference teams. Whilst I enjoyed it, I found myself wondering about those St Louis Blues. Then, to my delight, another Blues game popped up on television and that sealed the deal for me. I phoned my friend, Pam and told her that hockey was most definitely my game. I told her that I'd "found" my team. "The Kings, right?" was the reply. "Nope. The Blues". Stunned silence followed by "the..what?" Our friendship has never faltered even though our hockey loyalties are poles apart. Thanks to Pam I discovered hockey...and the Blues. Thanks to Pam, I travelled to stay with her in California and watched my beloved Blues play the Ducks and Kings on the road.

Sandra Pascoe
Penzance, England

Back in the mists of time, computing mags came with 3.5" floppy disks on the front, with various demos. One of them was 'Brett Hull Hockey'. A demo where you played as the Blues in one period, featuring CuJo, Craig Janney, Igor Korolev and the legend Brett Hull. I grew up near the ENHL Division 1 side the-then Medway Bears (now Invicta Dynamos), so I'd seen the odd game, but never played it at all. I played this one-period demo for ages on the school computers eventually wearing out the disk and a near-on 20 year love affair was born.

Grant Sales
High Wycombe, England

Jonathan Northall

Northwest Division

Calgary Flames

It was back in 2006 after the Turin Winter Olympics, I watched practically all the hockey tournament and by then I was keeping an eye on the NHL on Channel 5 and on nhl.com. I decided I needed to choose a team so I chose the Calgary Flames. I wanted to support a team that was Canadian simply because ice hockey is a Canadian sport and wanted to view a Canadian perspective on it.

Nigel Morris
Oldbury, England

My love for hockey started back in the 90's, when like a lot kids, my favourite film was 'The Mighty Ducks'. That film is what started it all. I would stay up all night playing NHL games with my best friend, watching the hockey on late night TV. This resulted in being late for school the next day and earning a couple detentions for my troubles. Those were the good times! This love affair lasted until around the time I finished school at 16 in 2003, and wouldn't be rekindled until 2008 when I started a snowboard instructor course out in Banff, Canada. During the season, I spent a lot of spare time in Calgary where I got an amazing feel for the city and just what hockey meant to everyone. I started joining in with the locals watching the games, playing hockey on the frozen ponds, getting involved in the chirping between fans, and then finally got to go to my first Flames game at the Saddledome. It was a battle of Alberta tie versus the Edmonton Oilers. What a first NHL game it was! Within the first 75 seconds of the game, there was a bench clearing brawl started by none other than Dion Phaneuf. It was a high energy game with the Flames winning the tilt 4-1, an experience I'll never forget. Since then there has been no looking back. I do my best every year to head out to Calgary to see my team through thick and thin.

Daniel Daw
Plymouth, England

My original interest for ice hockey stemmed from ice skating lessons from the age of 7 at the Basingstoke ice rink in the early 90s. Every week, I used to be taken to support the "then" Basingstoke Beavers now known as the Bison. I was absolutely enthralled by the sport and especially looked forward to the "Dunkin Donut" man between periods! In 2008, I spent four months outside Calgary training as a snowboarding instructor. It was that year and a whopping 14 years later that I got to see my favourite team play in the flesh. Since then I have made the 14,000km round trip several times to watch the Flames play over 10 games at the Saddledome.

Melanie Warn
Devon, England

The reason I support the Flames is because as a kid I loved wrestling. I was a massive Bret 'Hitman' Hart fan and, since he was from Calgary and was co-owner of the Calgary Hitmen of the WHL, he sometimes wore the hockey jerseys to the ring so I started just looking out for the Flames results in the newspaper and it started from there.

Raymond Jackson
Ballymena, Northern Ireland

Colorado Avalanche

For me it all started back in 1998. Everyone knew about the Avs in Sweden because of a player named Peter Forsberg: Number 21, Peter the Great, or as he is called back home "Foppa". He was already a living legend in Sweden by then. It is easy to believe that Peter was the reason for me to be an Avs fan but that can't be more wrong. My favourite player was Mats Sundin of the Maple Leafs and there were lots of other clubs to choose that had great Swedish players; Ottawa with Daniel Alfredsson and Detroit with Niklas Lidström and Thomas Holmström to mention a few. I really didn't care about the NHL before 1998, the year when my sister crossed the Atlantic Ocean and went to work as an au pair. She lived in Denver for 13 months and during that time I got really interested in the city. The Colorado Avalanche became a passion and if a player made me an Avs fan then I have to say it was Valeri Kamenski. I admired him for years even before he went overseas for the NHL. My sister later on sent me a postcard signed by Claude Lemieux and Adam Deadmarsh. My dad, who visited her in April '99, bought me an Avalanche jersey and from that period, the 98-99 season. I am an Avalanche fan and nothing will ever change that.

Mattias Boström
Stockholm, Sweden

I'm a fan of Peter Budaj and, recently, I went to Montreal to see Peter play.

Jonathan Northall

I saw my first NHL game with Peter in the net, it was a big dream. I have his actual playing jersey and one of his sticks.

Natacha Laporte
Strasbourg, France

I was ten years old in 2000 and my friend told me about the Colorado Avalanche while we were playing street hockey. I had no idea where to gather more information about this team without access to the internet. Finally, I found out some names of players and started to check results every day. I wasn't able to watch highlights. The Avs won the Stanley Cup in "my" first season as a fan and I was really happy. The internet and 'Pro Hockey' magazine have really helped me. It was all coincidence but I am now happy I have chosen this team, more aptly, that my friend from childhood did for me.

David Púchovský
Bratislava, Slovakia

After picking up a copy of NHL 2002, I needed a team. Unsurprisingly for an eleven year old kid I went for a team packed with stars. Back then Colorado had Sakic, Blake, Foote, Roy and my all-time favourite player: Peter Forsberg. The bond was sealed a couple of years later when I picked up an Avalanche jersey when on holiday in the US. The jersey has hung in every bedroom I've had since. In those ten years, the Avs have always played an offensive-minded brand of hockey too. Even in recent years where they've finished low down in the standings. There are many reasons to love this hockey club!

Mike Fuller
Newcastle, England

I'm from the town of Michalovce, Slovakia. Michalovce is about 8,857 km (5,504 miles) away from Denver, CO, the home of the Avalanche. So why follow the Avs? One day, my dad brought me a muesli bar and what we both didn't know was that they had little hockey cards in them. As I took the first bite, I felt something strange which wasn't muesli at all. In fact, I bit into one of those cards. It was a card of an Avs player, now I'm not sure if it was either Adam Deadmarsh or Adam Foote. Upon looking on it, I fell in love with the Avs. Actually, I just fell in love with the Avs jersey. The love for the team came after some time, with big help from my dad. He kept on buying me those bars. I actually found Roy, Hejduk & Sakic cards in them. Also, he started to buy hockey magazines for me. I used to look for every article involving the Avs, reading them over and over again. One of those magazines came with a big poster of Patrick Roy and the poster is still on my wall. In a way, the Avalanche players became my childhood heroes. And all that started with that one little card.

Michal Heely
Michalovce, Slovakia

Edmonton Oilers

Why am I am Oilers fan? Did I visit their arena first? No, that was Calgary. The rink itself? It's quite old but atmospheric. Their history? Wayne and all those cups? Possibly. Their fans? They are pretty wild. Their shirt? It is a cool logo. Their current roster? Ryan Smyth, The Nuge, Eberle; what's not to like? Their style of play? Been pretty exciting recently. Edmonton itself? They do have a very good shopping mall (complete with ice rink). More likely, perhaps, it's just a combination of lots of little things coming together at the right time in the right place (probably Wayne Gretsky Drive!!) making me an Oiler forever!

Joan Chisholm
Washington, England

The reason why is the very same as why I hate all those Manchester United, Liverpool, Chelsea etc fans who never actually go to see 'their' team...........because I saw them on TV. Back in the 1980's when I started to go to watch Solihull Barons, their chairman was Gary Newbon, the head of Central (TV channel) sport, and he had a weekly show featuring an NHL game. Needless to say that at the time the Oilers were about to become the most entertaining and best team in the NHL and so were featured regularly. So, you get familiar with the players and the style and become a fan by default. Even though for some time now they've been uncompetitive, they are still my team and every day I'm on their website to keep up to date. I've seen a number of games on the east coast of America, Toronto and London but never yet seen the Oilers.

Andrew Saunders
Birmingham, England

Jonathan Northall

Minnesota Wild

The reason I'm a Wild fan is because I like the logo and colours and it is the state where the "Mighty Ducks" movies were set. My favourite player is also Niklas Backstrom.

Vicki Morgan
Basingstoke, England

Vancouver Canucks

My story of becoming a Canucks fan started when I purchased NHL 10 video game for the Playstation 3. Purely an impulse buy at the time because I was not following NHL at all. At this point, I'd never watched a game at all, I just knew about the computer games. My choice of the Canucks came when I played the game and I didn't know anything about any of the teams. I scrolled though the teams until I found something I liked the look of. I saw "Canucks" and the orca logo and thought that was the team for me. I had no ideas about any of the players or even if they were any good. It wasn't till the end of the season I started noticing their results and thinking this team was pretty good.

Dan Birkin
Burton upon Trent, England

As a fan from Europe, you rarely have personal ties with a team. Your choice has to come from somewhere though. There are a couple of reasons in my case. First of all, I loved watching Swedish ice hockey teams on Winter Games back in the 90's plus I simply like Sweden as a country. Back in 2000-2001, the Canucks had a strong Swedish contingent and by strong I especially mean quality players: Markus Naslund, my favorite player of all times, Mattias Ohlund, the Sedins were enough for me to take interest in Vancouver. Back then, I had been playing one of the EA Sports NHL games and obviously chose Vancouver. Brendan Morrison and Ed Jovanovski joined the group of those I liked and admired. In other words, I belong to the group of fans who need certain players to admire, and then they decide which team they will cheer for. I love travelling and Vancouver resonates well with me as a place. I don't think I'd be able to cheer for a team from a totally boring place in the middle of nowhere.

Michał Pręgowski
Warsaw, Poland

Ice Hockey Nights in Europe

In 1996, I was on a market stall in North Manchester. Sat there, for a bargain fee of £3 was NHL96 for the Sega Megadrive. I'd never even heard of ice hockey before but for £3....why not? Over the next 6 months, I perfected my knowledge of players and the rules through the medium of Sega: icing, 2 line pass, cross checking etc. This is where I first became accustomed to the Canucks. I randomly selected a team to start my first season with and after skipping the Panthers (Florida have hockey? That's more absurd than hockey in Britain!). There lay the orca of Vancouver. After getting Bure and Naslund nearly 200 points between them, I was a Canuck. So, I actually tried the sport a few months after and despite nearly the whole of my team being Leafs or Rangers, I had to put up with, and still do, the silly hours to watch a live game in the Western Conference.

Dean Colasurdo
Manchester, England

Like so many things in life this passion is born from love....love for a boy. My boyfriend and I are from very different backgrounds, different ethnicities and different countries. His exotic accent, a mysterious charm and his undying passion for hockey drew me in. He would get up at 3am to do a fantasy draft with his friends, or watch his home team, the Vancouver Canucks, play even though we were 8 time zones ahead. In an effort to impress and, quite frankly, spend more time with him led me towards asking about hockey and why every Canadian is so crazy about this sport. The first few games we managed to catch I struggled keeping up with where the puck was; why were people only on the ice for one minute?; why do they keep dropping the puck at different places?; why are there four referees? Thank you hockey for being a little complex, I owe my relationship to you.

Joanne Turner
Leeds, England

I visited Vancouver in 2003 and found myself attending the opening night game against the Flames. My hockey knowledge was limited to say the least. By the end of the game, I was hooked on hockey and the Canucks were very definitely my team! I moved there in 2004 and, despite a lock out, I learned the game. So when the NHL returned, I was not only a 'knowledgable' hockey fan but a Canucks fan at the beginning of a new season in the franchise's history. Since moving back to the UK in 2008 I have spent countless late nights watching West coast games. I continue to search the schedule for East coast starts for the Canucks as it is only a five hour time difference. It feels slightly rebellious to support the 'most-hated' team in the NHL. For all these reasons, I am a Canuck.

Glenn Innes
Aberdeen, Scotland

Pacific Division

Anaheim Ducks

Quite simply, I am an Anaheim Ducks fan because of one man – Teemu Selanne. My family is Finnish and I spent a considerable amount of time in Finland growing up, where I learnt to both love and play hockey. Living in Helsinki, you chose between two teams: HIFK (who were my family team) and Jokerit (the new contenders). In the early 1990's, they created a very powerful team of young players, headlined by Teemu Selanne. I chose Jokerit partly to annoy my cousin and partly because they had a cool badge! I had seen Teemu before, but my first conscious memory of seeing how good he was came watching the 1995 Europa Cup (during the lockout) when he paired on a line with Jarri Kurri and Okatar Janecky. From that moment, I was obsessed with Selanne and you could say that my first NHL team were the Winnipeg Jets – however that only lasted a season before he was traded to the Mighty Ducks. This was when my true love of the NHL started. There wasn't much success for the Ducks at that point, however Selanne, Kariya and Rucchin were incredible to watch, and I fell in love with all things that 'quack'. My interest in the NHL actually waned when Selanne was traded (and the 2003 Stanley Cup final run bypassed me slightly). However, on his return to Anaheim I became more obsessed than ever. This coincided with Jiggy, Neidermeyer, Pronger, and a Stanley Cup! My love affair with the Ducks became even more powerful. A different generation of the Ducks now exist again, but I never miss a game (many replays unfortunately –you got to love the West Coast) and when the real 'Great 8' retires I doubt this will change much – his shirt will always reside in the rafters of the Pond soon anyway.

Allan Allison
Bristol, England

Dallas Stars

My father played a big role in allowing ice hockey to become one of my biggest passions. His job involves him going over to the United States a lot

Ice Hockey Nights in Europe

and he brought the game back across the pond to me. He took me to my first ever live game to watch my local side, Swindon, play in the English Premier League. I admired the intensity and high levels of action throughout the 60 minutes, something that sports such as football and rugby lack at times. I was about 6 or 7 years old but I still remember the occasion very well and I haven't looked back since with ice hockey playing a big role in my daily lifestyle. Having no real connections with the USA, choosing my team to support was simply a process of choosing. The Dallas Stars were one of the first teams I saw in an NHL game on terrestrial television and for some reason, I instantly connected with them. At a young age, perhaps, it was the name that interested me in them. Either way, I have supported the Stars for just over 10 years now and they hold a special place in my heart. After deciding that the Stars were a team for me, Mike Modano confirmed that. He is a role model to many and his high levels of skill, commitment and passion caught my eye straight away. His 16 seasons in Texas emphasise his admirable loyalty as well as being the highest points scorer by an American born player in league history also says a lot. Modano was certainly by role model growing up, I went on to play ice hockey at a decent level, playing the position of centre as well as being left handed, just like Mike himself. I have seen two Stars games over in the USA and I have a lot more planned in the coming years.

George Royle
Malmesbury, England

My team is the Dallas Stars. It has been for a long time too. My Dad was in the Royal Air Force when I was a kid so we did a lot of moving around when I was younger. When I was 5 years old, my Mother took my sister and I to Minnesota to essentially distract us from my Dad being based in the Falklands on a 6 month post. I don't really recall anything about the city itself nor the flight(s), hotels or a whole lot apart from my definition of a trip to the Motherland. The first game of hockey I ever saw was on that trip and I remember every touch of the puck, every smell of the arena and every name I saw on the backs of jerseys in the crowd. That night, the Minnesota North Stars were playing some team from Detroit with a crazy wheel thing on their chests. The whole thing, atmosphere, sounds, everything just had me hooked right from the first whistle until today and beyond. There was something about the way the North Stars played that night. In spite of the fact they were never particularly successful and facing one of the best teams of the time, they weren't intimidated. Their skating was fluent, sharp and relentless. They refused to give up even after going down by 2 by the end of the first period. That never say die attitude resulted in a 5-3 final score for Minnesota and a resounding lesson in how hard work will eventually reap huge rewards. I've supported the Minnesota North Stars ever since and the Dallas Stars as they became in the early 90's. I've followed every heartbreak, every resounding victory and have an unyielding faith in them that surpasses anything in my life (wife and children aside). They're the first team I look for, the heartbeat of my hockey obsession and even the reason behind my favourite colour. Bear in mind - due to my Dad's career - I've lived in Germany, Canada and all over the UK and the one thing that's always felt like home is the that game in Minnesota and wonderfully vivid memories of one night which ultimately created a monster.

Chris Bluff
Stockton-On-Tees, England

Los Angeles Kings

My name is Elina and I'm from Bulgaria in south east Europe. Hockey is not popular at all here but I really love the sport and my favourite team is the Los Angeles Kings. I've never watched a hockey game live and this is my life wish. I really want to move to LA so I can support my team there and live in this wonderful town.

Ivelina Toteva
Gabrovo, Bulgaria

I got into the Kings through a music video of all things, the music video for System of a Down's "Toxicity" featured their guitarist (Daron Malakian) wearing a 1998-2002 Kings jersey (Shield logo) and I thought it was a 'hell of a badass' looking jersey, not to mention the colours appealed to me as well.

Kenny Jones
Caernarfon, Wales

The Kings are my team because they are the first team I saw play live. It's kind of a rule I have with American sports teams, I follow the team I saw first, kind of like being "my home town team". I first watched LA at the O2 when they came over to play the Ducks, and I've been a Kings fan ever since.

Stuart Coles
Coventry, England

Ice Hockey Nights in Europe

Phoenix Coyotes

I support the Phoenix Coyotes because the feeling of belonging to a pack of supporters who stay behind their trusted warriors to go out onto the ice and face all that will challenge them. I went to Phoenix on holiday and fell in love with the place, people and the pack! When I first saw their jersey in a sports store, in a small town called Chandler, I fell in love with the famous Coyotes symbol (the howling coyote). I wanted to become a supporter of the NHL before I left on my holiday but could not decide which team to support. Once I had seen the Phoenix Coyotes symbol, I was sold! This was going to be my team and I was going to support them to the bitter end. That day in 2008, in a small mall in Chandler, I became a member of the Pack!

Ollie Jenvey
Isle of Wight, England

Who is my team? The Phoenix Coyotes! Not the most obvious or fashionable NHL team to follow but one I have my whole hockey life! I like to think my choice of the Coyotes reflects me as a person too: unique and willing to support the underdog. I think my choice of the Coyotes was made for me, I have always been into hockey and so has my family. My mother was the physio for our local club, the Altrincham Aces/Trafford Metros, the same organisation where I played junior hockey myself. Throughout the late 1980's and early 1990's I was regularly down at the converted aircraft hangar that served as the Aces/Metros home. Supporting them through thick and thin, through many years of no success, always the unfancied underdog. Naturally being a hockey nut I paid attention to the NHL and was able to catch the odd game on satellite TV, throughout my youth I hadn't really got an NHL team. It was during 1998 I believe, when I set up my first email account in an internet cafe in Wilmslow. The Phoenix Coyotes, descendants of the Winnepeg Jets, relocated to the middle of the desert in Phoenix. It intrigued me. I was fascinated by the city. Miles of desert everywhere surrounding a big city, miles of nothingness then skyscrapers! I loved the city, I loved the name and I loved the logo. In fact, the home shirt with the Kachina style Coyote was, and is, the only Coyotes shirt I own. I love supporting the unfancied, unfashionable Coyotes, I think it makes that bond stronger than any other in the NHL. I love talking to other Coyote fans in the US and in the UK. Like the team we support, it is a tight knit bunch, who appreciate having a team in the desert. It's been one hell of a ride since then, I always scour the schedules for Coyote games on the TV but, there usually aren't that many. I am passionate for the Coyotes, although I have never graced the America West arena or the Jobing.com I have vowed to attend a Coyotes game in the flesh.

Mark Woodcock
Macclesfield, England

My favourite team is the Phoenix Coyotes. I am a NASCAR fan and am named after one of the drivers. He died in 2001 but his son also races in NASCAR so I follow him, and he took his car on the ice in Phoenix. My friend got me into NHL ice hockey and started to watch Boston Bruins games so I thought that I needed to get a team to follow. I chose Phoenix and have been following since. I am relatively new to ice hockey and have only been watching for a season but I find it to be a very entertaining sport.

Dale Casson
Hull, England

San Jose Sharks

It was the 2010/2011 season where I first became a regular viewer of the NHL thanks to ESPN, but before that I'd always had an interest in ice hockey, mainly fuelled by an occasional visit to watch Milton Keynes Lightning and catching a few games during the Winter Olympics. As it happened, a coincidence between my football team (Fulham FC) and what is now my hockey team led to me pledging my allegiance to the San Jose Sharks. At first, I wasn't particularly 'picky' about which team to support, and tried to watch as many teams as I could. I wasn't sure if I should judge it on style of play, the club's history and tradition, or if I just liked their colours. Then one evening, I sat down to watch a game only to hear the commentator announce that the Sharks' goaltender would be Antii Niemi. Surely not the same Antti Niemi that played in goal for Fulham between 2006 and 2008? Predictably not, but the coincidence was too much for me to ignore and I made my decision that this was the team for me.

Adam Phillips
Luton, England

I am a diehard fan! The early NHL computer games co-incided with the birth of the San Jose Sharks and their entry into the NHL. The awesome name, logo and colours certainly helped as well. I still think we have the best logo in the NHL! I finally managed to get to the USA for a holiday in 2007 and saw my first game at the Shark Tank, sadly a 0-2 loss. Since then, I have seen the Sharks over 10 times (once in New Jersey) in 2008, 2009, 2010 and 2011 and shared the experiences with my wonderful wife who also is a Sharks fan now. Our first playoff game was a 0-4 loss but the atmosphere was mind blowing.

Jason Dunn
Woking, England

When I got into Hockey and the NHL a few years ago, I brought a copy of NHL 09 for my Xbox and chose the Sharks, mainly, for the reason I liked the name and logo! So I stuck with them as my team ever since.

Matthew de Bohun
Suffolk, England

Split Loyalties

Who is my team and why? If you know me you'd know this was a really hard question for me to answer. I can honestly say I have two teams. The Toronto Maple Leafs and the Pittsburgh Penguins. For me, both teams have always been there. I looked up to Mats Sundin, loved watching Jaromir Jagr play because those guys were the only ones making any kind of (rare) headlines here. I remember the VHS tapes I made after watching every single NHL game, because they were so rare. I watched them over and over again because it usually went a month or two without me getting a chance to watch a new game, any game. When I did get a chance to watch I was captivated by how the Penguins played hockey, they were always so talented but since I watched them they also had a mixture of grit and tenacity. The Leafs are a different story, I was always in awe of everything around that team. Maybe it's true I relate more to Canadian hockey fans and the way they follow the game. I always followed the history and the progress of the team but all the fan passion kind of shifted my feelings towards the Leafs a little more in recent years because I felt that this was the only proper way to follow a hockey team. All else in sports always seemed secondary, and that's exactly how I feel about my hockey team(s). So, if you want to categorize it, I'd say that a highlight reel fan, a fan of spectacular hockey in me always like the Penguins but the passionate hockey fan in me supported the Blue and White. That will never change.

Mislav Jantoljak
Zagreb, Croatia

Jonathan Northall

I started watching hockey in 2010 by coincidence. It was during the World Championship, where team Denmark was doing really well. At the same time, I had ESPN for free, for one month. The Stanley Cup playoffs had just started. The Philadelphia Flyers versus the Chicago Blackhawks! I was hooked, and watched all the games I could with an American friend living in Sweden. She watched from Örebro, I from Copenhagen, and we discussed it all on Messenger while watching. During the 2010/2011 season, I still followed the Blackhawks, and watched as many games as possible. I had been following an Islanders game with one eye, because of the fantastic Frans Nielsen on their team. The Maple Leafs seemed to play some fun hockey and had some good fights with some of the other Canadian teams. I remember thinking they were a really good team, winning so many games during the start of the season. But no one team, really got hold of me during 2011/2012. I watched a Leafs game with rookie Nazem Kadri, and he seemed like such a sympathetic player. He is the reason why I started following the Leafs and every time he got called up and did good, I felt so happy for him. Since I had been watching some Islanders games in 2010/2011, and the fact that they had a Dane (Frans Nielsen) on their team, I felt more drawn to them in 2011/2012.

Kristina Stryhn Laursen
Copenhagen, Denmark

Ice Hockey Nights in Europe

2 WHAT ARE THE HIGHLIGHTS AND LOWLIGHTS FOR YOUR TEAM?

It is the agony and the ecstasy of being a fan. We follow our team through the good times and the bad and this chapter is a collection of those standout moments. Whether it's silverware that is won or our fiercest rival beaten, the euphoria is immense. However, with those highs are the terrible lows. Each team goes through the doldrums at some point and we collect these nightmares too. Our memories of these events are subjective and I'm sure there are recollections in this chapter that are factually inaccurate. However, what cannot be argued against is the passion that emanates from these stories.

The pinnacle for any hockey fan would be a Stanley Cup win. There are many tales of fans reliving that great moment when their team wins Lord Stanley. One of my favourite moments as a Penguins fans was listening to a radio feed on my iPhone in a hotel somewhere that escapes me. I was sitting in the bathroom, to not wake my wife, when the Penguins beat Detroit in game 7 in 2009. The joy of winning was tempered by not waking people, including Mrs N. Also, the victories over divisional rivals resonate with fans far longer than other games. On the flipside, losses hurt. I think the infamous Islanders game on February 11 2011 is one that still hurts now. It was a terrible 9-3 loss plus an exhibition of everything that is bad about ice hockey. It even has its own Wikipedia page, such is the nature of that game.

Sometimes, it's hard to read criticism against your team. That's one thing I have learned through this book. I urge you to read critically but objectively. Perhaps put yourself in the position of the opposition to try and understand their view. Not working? Didn't with me either! Just move on to the next submission....

There are some obvious highlights and lowlights as a Ducks fan. You can't be a fan of this team without 'welling up' slightly at the memories of Paul Kariya scoring in game 6 of the 2003 Stanley Cup finals ('off the floor, on the board!!' – my favourite piece of commentary of all time), or the images after the Stanley Cup win in 2007 namely Teemu crying, and Giguere skating round the ice with his seriously ill son. Lowlights – well, see the first 6 years of franchise history, or the moment Paul Kariya announced he was going to the Avs. However, as a fan, smaller things sometimes seem to come to the fore. My personal highlights and lowlights both came in the 2010/2011 season – yet again another season where the Ducks started abysmally, then lit up on a crazy run to the playoffs. The highlight for me was in a game against Dallas, around 4 games from the end of the season, qualification for the playoffs on a knife-edge. We were 3-2 down going into the last minute and, after pulling the goalie, Teemu scores with seconds left. Cue wild celebrations! Then, into overtime, Fowler scores again and the team go crazy. I will never forget the image of a 40-year-old Teemu Selanne jumping and bunny hopping round the ice like an excited kid. That's what it's all about – that is the drama of hockey. Lowlight – same season in the playoffs. We are 40 seconds from taking a 3-2 series lead against the Predators then Shea Webber scores with a bomb from the point. The Predators inevitably win it in OT, and the series is effectively over, with the Ducks a broken team. 40 seconds away from victory in the game and series (likely) for it to be totally snatched away – that again is the drama of hockey.

Allan Allison
Bristol, England
Anaheim Ducks

Obviously, winning the Cup takes some beating as a high point, in terms of low points as a newish fan I can't say there have been any major ones, though finding out Tim Thomas was a Tea Party supporter was a bit gutting.

Richard Hardy
Hinckley, England
Boston Bruins

Last season, my highlight for the Boston Bruins has to be when we went undefeated through the whole month of November. We went from being the bottom team in the East, to the top. Always finding a way to win. We came back from 2 goal deficits; we put nine past the Flames, 6 past the Flyers. We were seemingly unstoppable, then we hit my "lowlights," the constant injuries started to pile up, and our play started to worsen. The loss of Horton devastated the team, his second concussion in 7 months, and the fact it went unpunished was horrendous. Then we lost Peverley to ligament damage, Ference, Bergeron, Pouliot, Mcquaid all missed games due to injuries.

Kimmi Noble
Sheffield, England
Boston Bruins

Ice Hockey Nights in Europe

I missed the highest highs and lowest lows of Sabres history. I didn't see them lose the Stanley Cup in Game 6 to the Stars on Hull's controversial "No Goal". I missed the 2 Eastern Conference final runs, including Pominville's OT short-handed game winner against Ottawa in the conference semi-finals. My highs and lows aren't quite as dramatic. The lowest points both involve Ryan Miller. First, was seeing him get taken out behind the net in 2009. A high ankle sprain to our best player pretty much single-handedly meant we missed the playoffs that year. I still to this day curse Scott Gomez for that. More recently it was Milan Lucic running over Ryan Miller. No matter what he says, that was a gutless move by Lucic and should have been a suspension. However, the worst part was not the hit. It was the Sabres lack of response to it. Years ago that would have meant an aggressive Sabres team would show some guts and backup their friend and star player. But they didn't. It was a low point for me and horrible to watch as a Sabres fan. The only high point came months later, beating Boston 6-0 in a physical game. High points so far have included seeing Ryan Miller win Olympic MVP and the Vezina Trophy in the same year as Tyler Myers exploded into the league to win the Calder Trophy. The highest point had to be the stunning win on February 13th 2009. On the night of the 12th, Flight 3407 had crashed into a house in Clarence, a suburb of Buffalo, where many of the Sabres players lived. 50 people lost their lives and the whole community around Buffalo was affected. After a moment of silence for the victims and their families the next night, the Sabres played a game against the San Jose Sharks at home. Despite getting two 3 goal leads in the game, the Sabres were trailing 5-4 at the end of the third. Then the Captain, Craig Rivet, tied the game with 3.4 seconds to go against his former team to allow the Sabres to go on and win in a shootout. The fairy tale ending was exactly what the Buffalo community needed and despite not being there, I could feel the emotions watching the game live. Definitely, a beautiful moment that I'll remember forever.

David Robertson
Aberdeen, Scotland
Buffalo Sabres

If there is one thing the Sabres stand for, it probably is mediocrity. In my three and a half years I have been following them now, there haven't really been a lot of big high or lowlights. We are always in the playoff race, sometimes we miss them and if we get in, we don't go deep. It gets frustrating, but also helps you not to build up too high expectations. 2011's playoff series against the Flyers had some pretty heart-breaking moments though. Losing game 6, which could've been the series-clincher, in OT after being up 3-1 and 4-2 throughout the game was pretty heart breaking. The team never recovered from it and we clearly lost Game 7. My personal highlight so far came only a few months after that in the Fall of 2011. The Sabres started their season in Europe and I got two tickets for their game in Berlin against the LA Kings and I took a weekend trip there with my Dad (including a cancelled flight and everything). We ended up winning the game and I finally got a chance to see my Sabres live, a really awesome experience!

David Trippler
Mainz, Germany
Buffalo Sabres

The top highlight, which is delivered almost every game, is watching Miikka Kiprusoff rob countless snipers of "sure" goals. The athleticism of this man always brings a grin to my face as he does the splits with a skate on each post and gloves the puck traveling up to 100mph from the air or diving full stretch back to the blue paint to make otherwise impossible stick saves. "The C of Red" is like no other fan base in the NHL sorry guys but it's true - everyone owns and wears the Calgary hockey jersey in or out of the Dome and in or out of the playoffs. The low lights are the inconsistency of goal scoring and continuity of team play. These two elements have been the team's downfall over the past 5 years. They've finally realised in order to restore the soul to win they must call up those hungry rookies waiting to be the next big star. Hoping for a brighter future to get our loyal veterans that cup!

Melanie Warn
Devon, England
Calgary Flames

My favourite moment as a Flames fan so far has to be the 4-0 demolition of Montreal at the 2011 Heritage Classic. To witness such a unique event, albeit from the comfort of my own living room on a small laptop screen, as a fan brand new to the sport was excellent. We played a great game that day despite the cold conditions and dominated a team who many expected to beat us. It's been a frustrating season for us this time around as we seem to love giving up leads, and being beaten in overtime or shoot-out situations.

Katy Parles
Newcastle-upon-Tyne, England
Calgary Flames

Ice Hockey Nights in Europe

The lowest points I remember are probably the late 90's & early 00's. Such a depressing feeling, checking the game scores week in week out....and being named one of the worst sport franchises in 2004. The highlight for me was the Stanley Cup winning season. Watching the likes of Toews and Kane drafted and establishing themselves as the core of this young team and winning the cup in such a magical way was amazing. I will always remember that moment: shock, happiness, excitement and tears.

Nathan Hollis
Norwich, England
Chicago Blackhawks

I will never forget the playoffs 2001. My father woke me up early in the morning and told me the result of the final 7th game. Colorado won. My next highlight for my team is the Eurolanche fan club. I established this organization in 2007. It was just small fan site like other over the web. Actually, I can say today I have been to Denver several times, visited many Avs games, met coaches, managers, players and many other people; I have even been in the locker room. Lowlights are definitely losses and especially losses in the playoffs. I remember when the Avs finished their road for the cup unsuccessfully and I really got ill so could not go to school.

David Púchovský
Bratislava, Slovakia
Colorado Avalanche

My personal highlight as an Avs fan isn't really a hard choice; I guess every other Avs fan out there who has seen it would choose the same. The date is the 9th June, 2001. The highlight being victory, against the New Jersey Devils, in game 7 of the Finals. The Avs dodged a bullet in Game 6, when the Devils had a chance to end it all, but were shut out by Patty Roy. The game was intense, I hadn't watched it live at that time (I was 6 years old at that time so staying up till night was a no-go obviously). I watched a re-run of it like a year or so later. The game itself was as intense as a Game 7 in the Stanley Cup Finals can get. The Avs getting on the board first, holding on to a 2-goal lead since the 2nd only to see it getting cut to one after Elias put one on the board. That's when it got even more intense. After getting one back, you could see the despair on the Devils' faces, desperately trying to get a goal. Shooting from almost everywhere only to be stopped time and time again by the great Roy.
And then, with 10 second remaining in the game, the score being 3-1, Garry Thorne shouted the epic "THE COLORADO AVALANCHE HAVE WON THE STANLEY CUP! RAYMOND BOURQUE – A DREAM

Jonathan Northall

HAD COME TRUE!"

Michal Hežely
Michalovce, Slovakia
Colorado Avalanche

The highlight is easy - reaching the play-offs in 2009. Despite being whitewashed 4-0, it was great to finally just be there and actually be relevant at that stage of the season. It was unfortunate that we had to play the defending champions, the Detroit Red Wings, and but for a dreadful 'too many men on the ice' call, we could have taken the series to a fifth game, but it was great just to finally get the monkey off our collective backs. As for lowlights, there are so many to choose from. But the one that stands out from the ocean of disappointment is our dreadful 2011-12 campaign. Hopes were high at the beginning of the season and the acquisition of Jeff Carter was a real boost to a team that felt it had a genuine chance of getting to the play-offs following a promising end to the previous season, but with just one win the first eleven games, our year was over by November. We finished last in the entire league and our talisman Rick Nash wanted out before the trade deadline, but ultimately stayed.

Steve McCaskill
Maidstone, England
Columbus Blue Jackets

As I am only 18 years of age, I haven't been following the Stars long enough to be a supporter when they last lifted the Stanley Cup back in 1999. Winning the cup is obviously the ultimate highlight for a lot of fans, but I still have my highlights. Just watching the Dallas Stars is a massive highlight for me. At around 1 in the morning, hearing the introduction music for Fox Sports Southwest gets me pumped and excited for each game, whether it is a playoff game 7 or a normal regular season game. Being a Stars fan has meant that I have seen some of the leagues greats play on a regular basis, both past and present. The likes of Joe Niuewendyk, Mike Modano, Brett Hull and Jere Lehtinen were all a privilege to watch and all had a massive impact upon why I admire the sport of hockey today. Hockey has changed quite a bit from when those guys were in their prime. Forwards are adding more and more tricks to their armoury every day and goaltenders are finding even more inventive ways to stop the puck. Watching players such as Jamie Benn and Kari Lehtonen in the modern game is something you just can't beat. Watching these players are the biggest highlights of my time supporting the Stars so far. There is one big lowlight that sticks out for me, and it is a pretty recent one. The 2010/11 campaign was a season of inconsistency which seems to be a common trend of late. After months of late nights, it came down to the last game of the season. A win would put us in the playoffs for the first time in 3 seasons, a loss would see us fail to reach the post-season. We were up against the Minnesota Wild at the Xcel Energy Center, a game I thought we should win quite comfortably. I was wrong, we lost, and I was forced to cheer on a team I didn't even support in the playoffs yet again.

George Royle
Malmesbury, England
Dallas Stars

The highest point for any fan of any NHL side has to be a Stanley Cup win. I consider myself very lucky to say I was engrossed in the Stars' entire playoff run in the '98-'99 season. When your team gets perennially booted out of the postseason in the first or second round, it's very easy to be flippant about the level of performance you have to maintain, just to get to the Stanley Cup Final itself. Game 6 of that final seemed to last forever with Eddie Belfour (the Stars' netminder at the time) and Dominik Hasek (then of the Buffalo Sabres) matching each other right the way through the contest. Shot after shot, save after save it was an absolute marathon of a game. Brett Hull scored the game winner (eventually) which to this day is widely contested in regard to its legality. The argument goes Hull had a foot in the goalies crease as he hits the puck to score. To be honest, whether he did or not, the whole Dallas roster had done so much for the franchise, the city and the sport itself in the local area since relocating from Minnesota, that any other result but a Stars win would've been gut-wrenching. Don't get me wrong, I feel for Buffalo fans and I know only too well it's still a bitter thing for them but whoever won that series, both teams put up an excellent fight and it's one of those series which made it a shame there had to be a winner. Where lowlights are concerned, pretty much every defeat stings. None were more painful though than the Stanley Cup final series between the Minnesota North Stars and Pittsburgh Penguins. The 1990-91 season had been a little disappointing where results were concerned but weak results from other teams led to the North Stars just scraping into the playoffs. In the first two rounds, they outplayed and frankly outclassed the two best teams that season in the St Louis Blues and Chicago Blackhawks in six games each. They then dumped out the defending champion Edmonton Oilers which booked their ticket to the finals. Quite the Cinderella story at the time and for the first three games at least, the North Stars put everything they had into pulling off one of the biggest upsets in North American sports history, taking a 2 game to 1 lead in the best of seven series. The Penguins eventually rallied and stormed away in game six with an 8-0 score which brought North Stars fans back down to Earth with an almighty thud. Two seasons later, the Minnesota North Stars would relocate to Dallas and certainly for the remainder of the 90's become a sheer powerhouse side in a much revamped NHL. That series defeat though is one that hurt like no other. The only thing like it that I've felt since was our run in the 2007-08 playoffs and the 6 game defeat at the hands of the Detroit Red Wings. After having proven critics and many fans wrong after series victories over the Anaheim Ducks and San Jose Sharks, the Red Wings were perhaps a step too far and we lucked out after 6 games. The postseason that term though was immense for our team captain, Brenden Morrow, in particular who dragged his team over hot coals for a lot of games.

That season wasn't to be for us though yet it still showed the true worth of a team from a non-traditional hockey market and what we bring to the NHL on a game by game basis.

Chris Bluff
Stockton-On-Tees, England
Dallas Stars

My biggest highlight was the Detroit Red Wings getting the record of most wins at home which was 23rd straight it was a huge feat by any sports franchise which is hard to replicate in the modern day with salary caps, draft picks etc especially with the record has been held over 2 decades. Lowest point was to see the home record finally come to an end after losing the Canucks a western rival 4-3 after the scored the winning goal in a shootout, not getting home ice for the playoffs only the second time in 20 years, which is a shock to many fans.

Junaid Hussain
Nottingham, England
Detroit Red Wings

Any team that has won the Stanley Cup has to have this up their highlights, but to beat the Penguins in game 6 in 2008, on their ice, was definitely a major high. Up there with that hard-fought win is winning back-to-back cups in the 90's. The massive rivalry with the Colorado Avalanche in the mid-90's, and the tension in those games is also fondly remembered. Lowlights are most definitely being beaten by the Penguins in 2009, this time in game 7, and then since that point, being taken out by the Sharks for the past two seasons. Also watching Jiri Fischer have a heart attack on the bench in 2005 was a shocking moment for everyone involved. The retirement of Steve Yzerman was also a very sad moment for all fans of the

Ice Hockey Nights in Europe

Red Wings.

Stuart Wilson
York, England
Detroit Red Wings

For me a huge highlight was being in Edmonton last year and watching Eberle score a sweet goal - his skill and the end result just left me amazed. The low - losing to Carolina in game 7, I was convinced we were going to get through.

Joan Chisholm
Washington, England
Edmonton Oilers

The highlights were the '96 playoffs where they got to the finals in their third year being an expansion franchise, was an achievement no one would have thought of. My favourite highlights must be Beezers play in the final game (game 4, 3OT) and were still 0-0 against a much more stacked team, the Colorado Avalanches. The lowlights have probably been the lack of playoff hockey - the longest drought in NHL history sitting at 12 years now (last time was 2000 playoffs). Also, seeing a lot of our stars leave for nothing because of the horrible front office. They waived a future 34-goal scorer in Grabner and let him go for a bag of pucks.

Dan Edlund
Stockholm, Sweden
Florida Panthers

For me the highs come with the amazing comebacks such as the Miracle on Manchester, or the Frenzy on Figueroa, though for my time as a fan, finishing dead last with Tampa Bay one year was the low point, and hitting the playoffs was the high point for me.

Kenny Jones
Caenarvon, Wales
LA Kings

Highlights - making the Western Conference finals back in 2003. Our first go at the playoffs and we made it to the final four. The WC final series ended too abruptly in 4 games, but felt that we had arrived in the league. Previous rounds were a wild ride going down 3 games to 1 in both series, only to comeback and win through. Personal one here: In 2010, I finally got to see them play live. Went to Tampere in Finland to see their pre-season warm up game against Ilves. We won 5-1 and one of my favourite players, Cal Clutterbuck got a hat-trick. Before the games I also got to see Greg Zanon and Mikko Koivu (another favourite) up close, they were playing keepy uppy and I got some decent pictures. Niklas Backstrom. Enough said. He can do no wrong in my eyes. Josh Harding is great to. I like goalies. We were the best team in the NHL in November 2011. Lowlights - losing Marian Gaborik to free agency. Our first true superstar and we got nothing back. It was a tough ask for Havlat to replace him and he never did. The Todd Richards era - we just never got going under him.

Vicky Morgan
Basingstoke, England
Minnesota Wild

Having only been a fan for a couple of years I can't give great swathes of detail here, although there are few moments that stick out to me. Highlights: 2010 Playoffs - beating the much more fancied Washington and Pittsburgh in 7 games whilst being the 8th seed in the East is certainly a highlight, the excitement and never die attitude across those 14 games got me hooked in hockey and I will certainly never forget them. P.K Subban: I just love watching this kid play, every time he touches the puck he can do something special, watch out for him to become a truly elite D-man in the next couple of years. Also, his hit on Brad Marchand in 2010 is simply unbelievable, probably my favourite ever. Lowlights: Max Pacioretty's injury. Injuries are a part of sport, but to witness a player breaking their back (C4 vertebra) on a dirty hit like that was disgusting. The fact it was a Bruins player who caused it made it worse, I don't think we will ever take appropriate enough action on the ice against Chara, despite the fact Max Pac has forgiven him off it. 2012 season - the less said about the season the better, we lead the NHL in man time lost due to injuries but that is no real excuse for how pitiful we played for most of the season. Finishing 15th in the East is not a moment to be proud of for a franchise that has so much history as a club and passion from the fans. From firing assistant coaches two hours before a game and not telling the players to trading Mike Cammalleri during the 2nd period of a game and sending him to a hotel in a taxi was a disgrace.

Daniel Betts
Coventry, England
Montreal Canadiens

Highlights and lowlights for Habs fans are quite drastic. One of the lowlights of this season has been last season. A team of Habs calibre at the bottom of the Eastern Conference (at the time of writing) is not something that any fan would expect of a consistent playoff runner. Other lowlights that often plague the team is some of the media attention around the team. Obviously the Canadiens live under the magnifying glass so there is a lot to deal with for the players. Also I think the team has drafted really poorly in of late. Yes we've got players like Pacioretty and Price show for it, but we haven't really drafted a superstar. As for highlights, there are many and I think one of the highlights for the team is its illustrious history. The Stanley Cup banners that hang in the rafters of the Bell Centre and the retired numbers of some of the games' absolute legends serve as highlights for the team.

A few years ago the playoff run that ended in the Eastern Conference finals was an absolute highlight. I remember recovering from knee surgery at the time and fighting the painkillers drowsing effects to stay up and watch the games and jumping up and down one legged as the Canadiens sank the Penguins. What a great spring that was.

Janne Virtanen
Hameenlinna, Finland (now Basingstoke, England)
Montreal Canadiens

Highlights are 24 Stanley Cups which is the most in the league but, alas, none since 92/93. Also, any win over the Leafs or the Bruins. Lowlights are Scott Gomez who is a total waste of $7million plus any loss to the Leafs or the Bruins.

Sharon Wedley
North Ayrshire, Scotland
Montreal Canadiens

I think the highlight and lowlight of the New Jersey Devils in recent memory has to be our whole season last year (2010/2011). We started the season with a new head coach in the form of John MacLean after Jacques Lemaire announced his retirement. Things didn't get off to a smooth start for MacLean, an NHL record of 9-22-2 meant that MacLean was consequently fired. This was definitely a lowlight of the whole organisation; the fans had wondered what had happened to our team. Lemaire was hired as interim head coach and immediately made an impact. The Devils turned their record around from 10-29-2 on January 9th to 32-32-4 by March 12th, a stretch of 22-3-2. What was even more amazing was that we were in with a shot of a playoff spot! In the end it was not to be. The Devils missed out and eventually finished 12 points behind the NY Rangers. So, in conclusion, that whole season went from being a total disaster up until January to one of the most memorable and outstanding second halves of the season. That is a perfect example of how proud the NJ Devils fans are of their team, they were with them all the way, through the tough times and the good times.

Andreas Tatt
Bristol, England
New Jersey Devils

For me the highlights of supporting New Jersey have to be the big hitting physical aspect of the team, that's one of the main reasons as a child I started following them. I also like the fact that in my opinion we have the best goalie to ever put on the pads between the posts and watching him you are always treated to some spectacular saves. And the final main highlight about being a Devils fan is our rivalry with the New York Rangers! Which is one of the fiercest in hockey.

My main lowlight of supporting the Devils so far has to be last season, absolutely shocking performance up to the all star break being in dead last and having Parise out injured also stung a lot, although we did turn it around the second half of the season and nearly made the playoffs in the end it didn't make up for such a disappointing start.

Gavin Clarke
Bristol, England
New Jersey Devils

Highlights: the Cup clinching goal scored by Jason Arnot in game 6 against Dallas in 2000 and the chaos on the ice in the following minutes. As many Devils fans do, I loved the A-line. Patrik Elias is one of my favourite Devils ever together with Scott Stevens, and both had the assists in that occasion....watching Scott lifting the Cup. The first Martin Brodeur goal in the playoffs in 1997, empty net, unbelievable... I've downloaded it from YouTube and still watch it laughing alone while watching. The Zach Parise goal (Jan 9th, 2010) against the Canadiens: incredible, and strongly wanted by the player.

Lowlights: I was in love (ok, I think still am in love) with Scott Stevens: one of the worst moment as a Devils fan is the day Scott retired. I couldn't believe I would not see him on the ice during games. I was, literally, in tears when I heard the news.

Another very sad moment came in July 2005 when Burnsie (Pat Burns) announced his retirement because of that evil thing that caused his death in 2010. I liked his way of coaching. Losing against the Canes in the playoffs in 2009 and it still hurts when I think about that game.

Emanuela Pozzi
Cernusco sul Naviglio, Italy
New Jersey Devils

Highlight - After three wins, we must win at New Jersey to secure 8th place in the East. Two goals from Richard Park placed us in 7th heaven but one second before the buzzer, the Devils tied the game and dropped us to deep hell. The game came down to a shootout. Dramatic. Our first two shooters would make their shots. We lead 2-1 when it came down to Sergei Brylin. He shoot and.... Wade Dubielewicz saved!!! We beat out Toronto by one point that season to make the playoffs. Lowlight - Islanders played in Raleigh and lost by nine goals! Never before had we lost by more than eight goals and we hadn't done that since losing 8-0 at St Louis in 1988. We took just 12 shots on Cam Ward, conceded three goals in every period. By the midpoint of the third, we had as many shots (8) as Carolina had goals (8).

Mikołaj Wójcik
Warsaw, Poland
New York Islanders

I would say the ultimate highlight of the Rangers would have to be the 1994 Stanley Cup win, including the Conference Finals guarantee and the Mark Messier guarantee! Since I've been watching the Rangers, I would say the highlight for me would have to be the 2012 Winter Classic victory over the Philadelphia Flyers at Citizens Bank Field. It was an incredible game cast in an unbelievable scene and what made it even better was the fact it was against the Flyers and they came back from 2-0 down as well! Plus the uniforms looked awesome as well! The lowlight for me would have to be when the Rangers missed out on the playoffs on the last day in 2010 against the Flyers. The fact that game went all the way to a shootout that made the loss even worse.

Daruish Gorgirzadeh
Bournemouth, England
New York Rangers

In terms of highlights, I guess my answer would have to be the 2011-12 season as a collective whole. Cup or no cup, it's been the most successful Blueshirts season that I have known. To top the Eastern Conference after a gruelling first month in Europe and Western Canada was very much unexpected, particularly after a few seasons of "will-they-or-won't-they" last-game dramas at the other end of the playoff positions. It's been a treat to watch what is now a largely home-grown roster develop together.

As far as lowlights go, I'd have to say Chris Drury's infamous late-show for the Buffalo Sabres during the 2007 conference semi-finals. For those that don't know (or remember), Drury tied the game with 7.7 seconds remaining in regulation. Max Afinogenov's overtime goal won the game soon after, and the Sabres rode their momentum through to a Game 6 win, sealing the series 4-2 in New York.

It still hurts to this day.

Alex Nunn
Romford, England
New York Rangers

The real highlight for me is seeing the Senators excel in the 2011-2012 season during a rebuild year. Watching a team do this well when many forecast them to be in the draft lottery makes me proud to support my team. As I have only really followed the Sens for a couple of seasons the only lowlight that comes to mind is seeing a few players leave that were a big part of the team which I had began to follow. Mike Fisher and Chris Kelly were players I enjoyed watching and was a blow to see them get traded, to Nashville and Boston respectively, in February of 2011 as part of the rebuild.

Robert Weaver
Gloucestershire, England
Ottawa Senators

My highlight is the Ottawa Senators beating New York Islanders, on their ice and getting in play-offs. My lowlight aren't all games where the Sens lost but there is one particular game, with the Penguins, where a female opera singer was the singing national anthem. That was really awful!

Elina Lazdina
Talsi, Latvia
Ottawa Senators

Well my highlights whilst following the Flyers have to be: the 2010 run to the Stanley Cup finals. Specifically, the Bruins series comeback from 3-0 down, game 7 comeback and "the shift" from Mike Richards against Montreal. I remember thinking after going 3 games down to the Bruins, that I would be content with the season if the Flyers won the next 2. That way they would have had a winning record for the playoffs after beating the

Devils in 5. For a brief period in the Montreal season, Flyers fans loved Michael Leighton. The shutouts after the highs of the previous rounds had us all believing it could be our year. On top of that we witnessed one of the greatest shifts in postseason history when Mike Richards human wrecking balled through the Canadiens to score into the vacated net. Sometimes you just have to scream the place down with excitement. Even in the early hours of the morning!

Another highlight has been seeing the recent progression in Claude Giroux. I became a fan too late to see Eric Lindros grow into the player he became, but it is fantastic to see Giroux turn into a superstar. There are exciting times ahead.

Lowlights: Well I imagine this could be quite common among Flyers fans. Goaltending. It is along running joke that the Flyers, up until this season didn't believe in goaltending. Since I started really following the Flyers in 1998, they have dressed 21 goalies. The ultimate lowlight with regards to goaltending was 'that goal'. The 2010 Stanley Cup winning goal. A goal that any NHL goalie should stop. Made even worse that the scorer, Patrick Kane, was taken 1st overall in the 2007 entry draft. The pick that in pre-lottery days would have been, by rights, ours. That being said 2006/07 an incredible lowlight. So much so that we Flyers fans don't talk about it.

Another lowlight would be Scott Stevens and that hit. Don't get me wrong, I love the big hits, and Stevens was one of the very best at it, but Lindros was never the same after that and we could only wonder what he could have still achieved. The hit changed him as a player. Trading Gagne to Tampa for spare parts hurt - a career Flyer and a personal favourite sent packing due to cap issues.

Ray Skeates
Basingstoke, England
Philadelphia Flyers

In my case, one certain highlight could be applied to both. Watching the Flyers compete for the Stanley Cup in 2010 against Chicago was a massively proud moment, but also watching them lose it in Game 6 was absolutely heart breaking. Coming back from 3-0 down in a Playoff series against Boston to win 4-3 in 2009/10 was incredibly special and Simon Gagne's overtime, game winning, goal in Game 6 of the 2004 Eastern Conference Final against Tampa Bay was also a hugely significant highlight.

As for lows, the 2006/07 season where we recorded the most losses and worst winning percentage in team history was a bitter pill to swallow. We even lost out on the draft lottery and had to pick 2nd overall. Ironically enough, the player who ended our Stanley Cup dream in 2010 was a guy we could have had if we won the lottery and picked 1st overall in 2007: Patrick

Kane.

Dave Lidbury
Bristol, England
Philadelphia Flyers

My highest point for the Phoenix Coyotes was seeing the captain, Shane Doan, finally getting a hat-trick after so many 2 goal games. He is my favourite player for the Yotes and a great captain. My lowest point for the Phoenix Coyotes was seeing them get swept 4-0 in the 2010/11 playoffs by the Detroit Red Wings. The last game being played at home and they still couldn't stop Detroit scoring.

Ollie Jenvey
Isle of Wight, England
Phoenix Coyotes

The highlight of my Pens supporting career so far was definitely the Stanley Cup win in 09. I'm not sure I had many nerves left by the end of the third of that game! Lowlight? Those few dark years before Sidney Crosby or the Stanley Cup Final in 2008, I definitely thought they had a chance after making it all that way and was worried they'd struggle to make the final two years in a row! (How wrong I was)

James Bird
Burnley, England
Pittsburgh Penguins

My highlight and lowlight both came within a year of each other. The highlight would have to be when the Penguins won the Stanley Cup in 2009. It was game 7 against Detroit and it needed a last second save from Marc Andre Fleury to secure the win - those last few minutes were the longest of my life! It was an amazing feeling after the previous year, which was my lowlight. It was when the Penguins lost in the final against Detroit: to get that close to the cup and not win was heart breaking.

Tom Harding
Isle of Wight, England
Pittsburgh Penguins

Highlight was that game 7 of the 2009 finals when Penguins won the Stanley Cup beating Detroit Red Wings in Detroit. I remember watching the game with couple of my friends, who were Red Wings fans. I don't think I will ever forget those 6.5 seconds before the last horn sound and Flower's save. Lowlight was probably the 2010 playoff game 7, a 5-2 home loss to the Montreal Canadiens, in their last game in Mellon Arena. It was a huge disappointment the way they played that game.

Sanja Prošek
Ljubljana, Slovenia
Pittsburgh Penguins

Having started my support of the Pittsburgh Penguins on the high of a Stanley Cup win it would be prudent to say that all else after that point would qualify as a low, however, since then there has been the great 2009 season where the Penguins got back at a seemingly dominant Red Wings team to take the Stanley Cup in 'Hockey Town'. The sprawling dive of Marc-Andre Fleury with 2 seconds on the clock will forever be the greatest of the great moments for me. As for the low it would be normal to pick a time where your team was in a slump, and as all Pens fans know we have had a few of those over the years. Also, times where your hockey season ends early leaving you with the predicament of 'do I love the game enough to watch another team lift the cup?' Mine, however, would have to be the lockout of 2004-5. Early on in my support of the Penguins I was subjected to the concept of a lockout, 1994-5 to be precise. Being brought up on UK sports, the idea that a whole season could be cancelled due to a labour dispute was entirely foreign, but as a fledgling supporter my time was filled with other things. For the NHL and the NHLPA to allow this situation to happen again was an immensely confusing event for me. How could two sides of a discussion get to a point where the only option was to deny millions of fans their sport, hundreds of players a chance to play and the thousands of people employed by the franchises a chance to earn a living?

Rob Aherne
Stafford, England
Pittsburgh Penguins

In Sharks history, many would pick the upset playoff victory as 8th seed over 1st seed Detroit in 1993-94 as a major highlight and clearly our 3 Western Conference Finals appearances in 2003-04, 2009-10 and 2010-11. Those losses could also be the lowlights of course as we failed at the last hurdle :-(For me though, the highlight was our trip in 2009-10 - 5 games, 5 wins: 5-2 v Ducks, 3-2 s/o v Coyotes (my first NHL shootout), 5-2 v Capitals (with Ovi), 3-2 s/o @ Coyotes (on TV in Player's Sports Bar at Pier 39 in San Francisco) and 4-1 v Oilers. Lowlights - losing 0-2 and 2-4 on my first trip in 2007 and 1st playoff game 2010-11 lost 0-4.Hang on though, despite that loss, hearing the whole crowd shouting 'BEAT L.A.' was worth it!!!

Jason Dunn
Woking, England
San Jose Sharks

Highlights: Seeing Wayne Gretzky sign for us in 1996, I was so excited! Also, the run that took us into the 2009 Stanley Cup playoffs, Chris Mason was a wall and we really shocked everyone. The 10-3 win over the Red Wings at Joe Louis was one of my all-time favourite scores and days of my life! The 'Monday Night Miracle' against Toronto. Watching Grant Fuhr play. Lowlights: Getting swept by San Jose in the first round of the 2000 Stanley Cup playoffs, after being the President's Trophy winners that season. Mike Keenan's entire reign, trading away Gretzky and losing Hull because of Mike Keenan, Mike Keenan, Watching Nick Kypreos destroy Grant Fuhr's knee in the playoffs, oh and Mike Keenan....

Grant Sales
High Wycombe, England
St Louis Blues

The highlight for me was getting to see Tampa Bay in the Eastern Conference final live. It just happened that the holiday we booked coincided with Tampa reaching the final which I didn't think would be possible during the season. Getting the Pens and Caps in the first two rounds meant I didn't hold out much hope! The lowlight of following Tampa was when the organisation was having ownership/financial issues and we lost John Tortorella, Brad Richards, Dan Boyle but I guess Stamkos was the good that came from it!

Alan Giles
Reading, England
Tampa Bay Lightning

I can imagine that for many Lightning fans their highlight is most likely the 2004 playoffs when the Lightning won the Stanley Cup. Sure, I cherish that very much too, but given the fact I didn't get to watch any of those playoff games (mostly due to my very limited access to the internet and the lack of knowledge of English) I must name a different moment in Lightning history that is a highlight for me – it is the 2011-12 season and everything about it. Starting with the new owner Jeff Vinik, new GM Steve Yzerman, new coach Guy Boucher, new players, followed by new uniforms, reconstruction of the Forum and last but not least the return to the Stanley Cup playoffs. The whole playoff run was absolutely amazing and I won't ever forget the comeback against the Penguins and the sweep of the Capitals. Too bad it ended with a loss to the Bruins. As for the lowlight for the Lightning....the whole era that preceded the current Lightning situation. The era of Oren Koules and Len Barrie. Barry Melrose fiasco. Non-stop trade rumours surrounding Vinny Lecavalier etc. I would like to forget all of that because it was plainly painful to witness as a fan.

Katerina Brzonova
Zlin, Czech Republic
Tampa Bay Lightning

Being a Leafs fan, there have been far more lowlights than highlights over the last couple of decades, however my highlight is without doubt the 1992-93 playoff run to the Campbell Conference final. Within that playoff run there were several highlights in their own right - Nikolai Borschevsky's Game 7 OT winner at Joe Luis Arena to beat the Wings, Doug Gilmour's tantalising wraparound goal vs. St. Louis, and Dave Andreychuck's 50+ goal season all stand out as memorable moments. As for lowlights, there have been many including Sundin leaving to go to Vancouver, however my lowlight for my team has been the lack of a playoff team for years. For a franchise of that stature to be in the playoff wilderness for so long is simply a travesty for hockey.

Christopher Barr
Dungannon, Northern Ireland
Toronto Maple Leafs

My highlight in my 12 years of a Leaf fan came in the 2001/2002 Playoffs. After seeing off the New York Islanders in a brutal and long 7 games series, the Leafs then faced their bitter rivals Ottawa for a Conference Cup Semi Final "Battle of Ontario". The Leafs were never ahead in this series which was violent from start to finish, with no love lost between the two sides. Coming back from a 3-2 deficit to win the series 4-3 was very sweet, especially after all the talk from Ottawa that they were going to finish this series off in their favour. My lowlight came in the 2011/2012 season. On February 11th 2012, the Montreal Canadiens were to play the Toronto Maple Leafs at the ACC. Before the game the Leafs honoured former captain Mats Sundin by raising his number 13 to the rafters. A great ceremony however was marred by a truly pathetic and uninspiring performance from the Leafs and after shelling 4 goals in the 2nd period, lost 5-0 to our bitter rivals. This awful performance led to a real spiral in results and the eventual firing of coach Ron Wilson.

Mark Rackham
Kent, England
Toronto Maple Leafs

Highlights? In person, being at my first Leafs game in New Jersey on New Years Eve 2005, seeing players like Mats Sundin, Tie Domi, Darcy Tucker and Ed Belfour, who have since retired, with the Leafs winning 6-3. On TV? Difficult for a fan of a team who haven't made the playoffs for so long! But I'd say any win over Montreal is special! Lowlights? In person, being at the Air Canada Centre for the game against the Habs in 2009, the Leafs couldn't make the play offs, so there were loads of Habs fans, they took a 4-0 lead and went on to win 6-2. I was gutted! On the bright side, I saw the Leafs win at New Jersey (again, but new arena) a few days later. On TV? Every time we lose to the Habs!

Jamie Mash
Northallerton, England
Toronto Maple Leafs

Highlights: For me the biggest highlight was getting to the Stanley Cup Final is 2011. The team thoroughly deserved to get there after winning the Presidents Trophy. Unfortunately it wasn't to be in game seven, but I see this as something to build on. This should give the players something to look at they made it to the line they just need to get there again and get over the line. Hopefully this will be sooner rather than later. Lowlights: It would be obvious of me to say losing game 7 is a lowlight but to me it can't be looked on negatively there's teams in the NHL who would kill to be in the Stanley Cup finals, so we can't dwell on one defeat. There's teams like Montreal and Toronto who are really struggling just to make the Play Offs the Canucks are in a good position for another real challenge in the next couple of years, the future is bright.

Dan Birkin
Burton upon Trent, England
Vancouver Canucks

The lowlight for me was without doubt game 7 of the Stanley Cup.
I don't think any explanation is really needed. A whole city rioted because of it!
My personal highlight was Canucks at the Ducks on 30th Dec 2011.

Ice Hockey Nights in Europe

Canucks won 5-2. Why's it a highlight you ask? Because it's the only game I've seen in person!

Dean Colasurdo
Manchester, England
Vancouver Canucks

The Canucks are well managed and I absolutely love that. Mike Gillis is a mastermind of a GM; I like people who think outside of the box and he (and his team, especially L. Gillman) tends to do that a lot. The "Moneyball" reference may be a bit overused these days, but I really like it when "my" GM is a thinker and has a rather scientific approach rather than basing on feelings, hunches etc. The highlight of the team is the team itself, too. Apart from the 2007-2008 fiasco, the Canucks are doing very well for almost a decade. The Gillis era is a joy to watch. Four consecutive 100+ point seasons say it all, to be frank. The lowlights? I guess I have to say the fans and the media from Vancouver. Greatness is often accompanied by madness. Some people don't have a clue. Some are delusional. Some are hysterical. And some of the local media feed off it. Not happy when they blow things out of proportions and that happens in Vancouver sometimes. That's frustrating. Also: I did not particularly like some of the embellishment from 2011 playoffs. What really annoyed me was that Boston-centred media turned on a scheme to show Canucks as gutless and cheap and embellishing, while a quick YouTube search for flicks from the very same playoffs would show you many players from many teams embellishing. This was not Vancouver's thing and I'd rather have my team stop doing that. If you don't want a certain reputation, you need to stop doing things that reinforce it. There is still some embellishing; I don't like that, especially from established point-getters like Ryan Kesler or Alex Burrows.

Michał Pręgowski
Warsaw, Poland
Vancouver Canucks

A highlight that stands out is winning the Winter Classic in Pittsburgh. I'm sure most people thought that the Pens would win given their form in the lead up to it so to win was great. Being in the Winter Classic also meant we got featured in HBO's '24/7 The Road to the Winter Classic' which gave me a great insight into the team behind the scenes. Lowlights, apart from every loss, are mainly that every year has ended in disappointment in the post season. The worst feeling that I can remember was the 2009/10 season getting knocked out in the 1st round to the Montreal Canadiens after such an amazing regular season. We'd had a tough loss the year before in game 7 to the Penguins but winning the Presidents Trophy so easily that season meant I was full of optimism for the playoff run and we got knocked out to the lowest seeded team in the first round.

Hana Imiolczyk
Merthyr Tydfil, Wales
Washington Capitals

For the lowlights: That tragic overtime loss to Philadelphia where Pavelec made 50 saves including one of the saves of the year, but the Flyers managed to tie it up with 10 seconds left and Jagr scored the overtime goal. It was horrible. I get a little too emotional so I cried for hours. That was so disgustingly disappointing I still can't talk about it. And the loss to Ottawa Senators. We tied it up with 3 minutes left, just a lucky bounce off of somebody's hand, they had to review it and what not, but it was a goal and everybody was so happy. And like 20 second later Ottawa scored. The worst thing about this game was that it was the game that basically sent us out of the playoffs. I had to go to school right after the game and I was tearing up the whole time. And the highlights: First of all, the Jets being back home. I know I have never even been to Winnipeg but as I see the fans I'm so glad they moved and extremely happy for the city, it's amazing. In terms of games I have to say the 7-0 win over the Florida Panthers, that was really important game with division rival and nobody expected this. Also the 2-1 win over the Bruins was pretty neat. And I really loved the 4-3 overtime win over the Washington Capitals where we went from 3-goal deficit in the middle of the game to a beautiful goal in overtime. And our fourth line was on fire!

Štěpánka Černá
Dolní Němčí, Czech Republic
Winnipeg Jets

3 WHICH TEAM OR TEAMS DO YOU LOVE TO HATE?

The definition of hate is to "dislike intensely or passionately; feel extreme aversion for or extreme hostility toward; detest". For some, it is the obvious reaction to a team. They are the archenemy. As a true fan of YOUR team, you are duty bound to hate THEM. What is peculiar about this mentality is that it transcends the Atlantic Ocean. In my case as a Pittsburgh Penguins fan, the thought of the Philadelphia Flyers fills me with a certain feeling of revulsion. So ingrained in my psyche, the response is almost Pavlovian. However, I've never been to either city. In fact, I've never set foot in Pennsylvania but the Pens-Flyers rivals burns deep in my small part of England. I am also aware that the feeling is very much reciprocated by Flyers fans this side of the Atlantic.

As I read through submissions for this chapter, I couldn't help but notice that the vicarious hatred of teams was rife. However, some found that a player would be the catalyst for their hatred. Perhaps a less than legal hit or a game winning goal to beat your team; whatever the reason, the vitriol was evident. This is not a feeling that is unique to ice hockey. Most sports are proliferated by this thought process but I find that it is the intensity that is more distinctive.

I think sometime as a remote based fan you do lose some of the intensity of local rivalries. Yeah, I quite want the Kings to lose, and I always like beating the Red Wings, however the teams I hate are normally the ones that repeatedly beat us. On that note – the only team I genuinely hate in the league are the Nashville Predators. The 2011 series has a lot to do with it; however we just can't beat them. I now cringe even if I hear their name, or see that mustard yellow, or see the face of Shea Webber when yet again he has Getz and Perry in his pocket. They should be a team I like with their workmanlike hockey ethos and building a franchise out of nothing. However, I despise them, their fans superiority complex over us, and the fact they always beat us!

Allan Allison
Bristol, England
Anaheim Ducks

Vancouver Canucks for the injury they gave to Nathan Horton in the 2011 Stanley Cup playoffs.

Amy Hill
Camberley, England
Boston Bruins

After the epic final series of the Stanley Cup finals, I loathe the Vancouver Canucks. The Sedins are so talented, but will not stand up for each other. What kind of player stands there while a 5 foot 8 inch agitator (Marchand) ragdolls and punches them in the face repeatedly, only to use the excuse, "I was gonna keep letting him punch me so the referee would see and sort it out?" I also cannot stand Burrows. Biting Patrice Bergeron then denying it when it's on camera! Also, the fact that Luongo tried to make jibes about Tim Thomas then proceeded to concede goals from every single Bruin, and got pulled in 2 of the games.
I know as a Bruin fan, I should hate the Habs as well....

Kimmi Noble
Sheffield, England
Boston Bruins

The teams I love to hate would be the Toronto Maple Leafs, Boston Bruins, Montreal Canadians and Philadelphia Flyers. I love to hate all of them because it's just been that way growing up especially the Leafs one, and the Boston one got worse after Milan Lucic ran and injured Ryan Miller.

Gareth Dutton
Manchester, England
Buffalo Sabres

Most fans probably dislike the other teams in their division the most and I'm no exception there. My number one hated team is the Leafs. Not because of their team, their current roster doesn't frighten anyone, but because of their incredibly high amount of obnoxious fans. I know about tradition but more fans a franchise has then the more idiots you will find amongst them. However, for the Leafs this idiot-to-normal-fan ratio seems extraordinary high. In all hockey forums I visit, it's almost always the Leafs fans that strike me as the most dislikable. Add the often Leafs-centric coverage in the media, and the Brian Burke factor, and you've got yourself a franchise that's pretty easy to hate.
No other team from the Northeast Division really comes close. I don't like

the Canadiens' sense of entitlement and the media focusing on them so much, but they have decent and knowledgeable fans. I don't like some of the players on the Senators and the Drury-incident from some years ago still is a factor but don't really have a problem with the franchise or the fans per se. Last but not least are the Bruins who have some despicable players and one of the worst hockey personalities ever in Jack Edwards.
At the end of the day, I envy them for their team. The only team that might come close to the Leafs are the Flyers, mainly because of their fans as well, but we don't see them nearly as often as the Leafs so I don't perceive their 'unlikeability' as strong as the Leafs.

David Trippler
Mainz, Germany
Buffalo Sabres

There's only one team I truly despise in the NHL and that would be the Oilers. Without the "Battle of Alberta" being a consideration the past five years, Edmonton have proven time and time again that they prefer tactics such as diving and faking injury as if there were snipers in the roof tops. The fans have shown an equal amount of dishonour by using blinding lasers during match ups with the Flames. Not meaning to tar everyone with the same brush but I really am still looking to come across decent Edmonton players and fans.

Melanie Warn
Devon, England
Calgary Flames

To answer your question, I love to hate Buffalo and Washington. The Buffalo rivalry dates back to the playoffs a couple of years ago, and the chirping between fans both before and after games are often priceless and fun to be a part of. At the same time, there's no team I like to pound more than the Sabres. And the fact that they haven't won a cup in forever is just brilliant. Another team I love to hate is the Washington Capitals, but that is mostly because they're a fierce division rival.

Thomas Olsen
Oslo, Norway
Carolina Hurricanes

Have always had a soft spot for the Oilers....they have an amazing history. Gretzky, Messier, Coffey; a real Canadian dynasty. As for teams I hate....Vancouver as of late. Since the emergence of the 2008 Blackhawks, the two have had some immense battles and a real fiery rivalry has emerged. Obviously the Red Wings rivalry is big but for me personally it's the Canucks.

Nathan Hollis
Norwich, England
Chicago Blackhawks

I don't really love to hate any team, but there are 3 teams I really, really dislike: Vancouver Canucks, Washington Capitals and Philadelphia Flyers. I don't like the policies of these three teams at all. They frustrate me and annoy me. I don't love to hate them, but I hate them. When there's a guy like Alex Ovechkin in your team, I cannot possibly like your team. I really hope 'Ovi' never becomes a Blackhawk. And no, I'm not a Crosby fan. Ovechkin is in my opinion extremely overrated player. When you play, you play for your team. Not for yourself. I like players like Marian Hossa, Patrice Bergeron, Teemu Selänne and Brent Seabrook way more. They're true team players and lead by example.

Satu Vanhanen
Joensuu, Finland
Chicago Blackhawks

I hate the Rangers. They have a great history and are rightfully a premier club, but the fact they sign so many amazing players and completely ruin them by not giving them playoff hockey. The list is endless: Gretzky, Lindross, Bure.... It looks like finally they have a good team and should be nailed on for success, but by not getting the best out of some of the star players they have paid big bucks for is disappointing.

Andy Parsons
London, England
Colorado Avalanche

Detroit Red Wings, definitely. No question for me. I am an Avs fan. I was born to hate the Red Wings. The rivalry has been created in 1990's. The great all-stars and future members of hall of fame were fighting in hard games for the honour of the Avalanche organization. They had to face ugly incidents and played hard as they could. I know many fans, mostly from Detroit, which do not think the rivalry is continuing these days. I do not support this opinion. There is also Vancouver Canucks.
To be honest, I have heard more bad words about this team from other fans than about Detroit. Vancouver is probably most hated team by other

fans.

David Púchovský
Bratislava, Slovakia
Colorado Avalanche

I guess that the correct answer would be the Red Wings but I have actually liked them over the years. My aggressions have instead been pointed against Dallas Stars and Edmonton Oilers. During my first years as a supporter of the Avalanche, they had lots of battles against the Stars. They met during the regular season in the Western Conference fighting for top spot but they also met in the playoffs. In the 1998-99 postseason the Dallas Stars won the Conference Finals by 4-3. I think that it was then that my emotions started to boil. The Stars went on to win the Stanley Cup. A title I thought belonged to the Avs. The year after, the first playoffs of the new millennium, history repeated itself. The Avs lost once again in the conference finals by 4-3 to the Stars. The best thing that year was that Dallas later on lost against the Devils in the Stanley Cup finals. In 2001, the Avs won the Stanley Cup but never met the Stars in the playoffs. Who knows how that would have ended? The Oilers, on the other hand, weren't really a big rival but they had some kind of capability to beat the Avs even if they were a team struggling on the lower half of the table. They could come from a defeat against the league's worst team and wipe the floor with the Avs the following night as I remember it. When that happens a couple of times against the same team, not as good as the Avs, you begin to dislike them a lot.

Mattias Boström
Stockholm, Sweden
Colorado Avalanche

As an Avs fan that's an obvious one. I love to hate the Detroit Red Wings. We'll kinda.... I hate to admit it, but the hate is more something manufactured, something artificial which didn't come naturally. Don't mistake me here, I hate the Red Wings, but I kind of had to be helped to do so. The reason being that the Avs-Red Wings rivalry was most intense in the 1996-2001 era when we met 5 times in the play-offs. I was born in 1995, I'm glad that I can recall the 2001 Cup memories. After 2002, the rivalry is mostly something for the old timers, something the younger fans find hard to do because they don't have those reasons the older fans have for hating them. The other team I really dislike is the New Jersey Devils. Why? Well, one of the reasons being the endless Roy-Brodeur (Roy being my obvious choice!) talk about who's the better goaltender. It may sound silly, but it really gets annoying and since I'm stubborn as it gets, I'll always be the one saying that Patty Roy is the best. The other reason is the fact that I have 3 friends that are Devils fans and we like to argue about almost everything. Most recently the topic was the Avalanche's failure to get into the post-season, at which I just smile and say "Just wait for the next season guys....we'll be a contender, you'll be a rebuilder".

Michal Hežely
Michalovce, Slovakia
Colorado Avalanche

Like many Avalanche fans, I'm not too fond of the Detroit Red Wings, I'd love for the rivalry to get back to the ferocious level it once was. I would say part of the reason I don't like them is envy, how do they manage to be so good every year? Nobody likes a team that always wins. They didn't help themselves when they went out and signed cheap shot extraordinaire Todd Bertuzzi either.

Mike Fuller
Newcastle, England
Colorado Avalanche

The Detroit Red Wings are perhaps my most hated team. Success breeds contempt, perhaps some would say envy, and the whole 'Hockeytown' sense of superiority adds to the ill-feeling. Being a Green Bay Packers fan in the NFL (who label the city 'Titletown'), I'm not a fan of Detroit sports teams anyway. The Packers twice-yearly matchups with the Detroit Lions in the NFC North are fiercely competitive. The fact that the Red Wings defeated the Blue Jackets in our only play-off appearance to date doesn't help either. The Nashville Predators are another team that I love to beat. A divisional rival and only two years older than the Blue Jackets, they are a team by which Columbus can measure its success and at the moment, we compare unfavourably.

Steve McCaskill
Maidstone, England
Columbus Blue Jackets

I would love be a doe-eyed romantic and say any team who plays the sport deserves every ounce of credit they get. Sadly, romance ends with the Detroit Red Wings. This is the club against whom the Dallas Stars have continued (until very recently) to be absolutely dominated, torn to shreds and usually thoroughly humiliated, regardless of the building or the situation. I want to say I have a respect for them for being 'another team in the NHL' and I get no joy from despising them as fiercely as I do. The Wings were the team I saw my beloved Stars (or North Stars as they were at the time) play in the first game I went to. Even in that game there seemed to be arrogance about them, carrying themselves around the rink as though they had a right to win the game without protest and it's exactly that kind of attitude I can't bear. They are now the reason I get a shudder when I am given a cup of coffee in a red mug, the reason I will never use a red pen and the reason that I don't necessarily hate any former Stars who go to play for them... they're merely left to sleep on the couch. P.S: There's no denying they do have the coolest jerseys in the league though.

Chris Bluff
Stockton-On-Tees, England
Dallas Stars

The team I would say I love to hate the most would be the San Jose Sharks. This is because they seem to be a team that has the Red Wings' number, especially in the playoffs. Every time the teams play, it is certainly a great game, but the Sharks seem to have the Wings' number, when it matters the most. Whilst I love to hate the team, however, I have a lot of respect for them. Another team I love to see fail is the Pittsburgh Penguins, mainly due to Sidney Crosby. As great as he is on the ice and as a player, something about him frustrates the life out of me, though it's hard to pick out a particular reason as to why, I just love to see Crosby get knocked around and his team fail. There's no real, great, detailed reason for this, I guess it's just how I've taken to Crosby himself.

Joe Alderson
Stoke-on-Trent, England
Detroit Red Wings

San Jose Sharks - non division rival beating us twice in the conference semi-finals in consecutive years a team which has the better us. Chicago - stopped us winning the 2010 division title which hurts and both being part of the original six so the history of the rivalry is huge like the Packers and Bears in the NFL.

Junaid Hussain
Nottingham, England
Detroit Red Wings

Jonathan Northall

The Red Wings rivalry with the Colorado Avalanche is well documented. Through much of the 90's the teams were at each other's throats over an incident involving Claude Lemieux and Kris Draper. Now, however, the teams have changed so much that the rivalry is no longer as fierce as it was, yet many fans who remember those days still hold a torch of bitterness for the Avs. Way back in the Original 6 days, and in geographical terms, the Toronto Maple Leafs was Detroit's biggest rivals. Despite Toronto's lack of competitiveness in the playoffs for many years, there is definitely a massive atmosphere at Leafs versus Red Wings games which still gets both fans and players fired up.

Stuart Wilson
York, England
Detroit Red Wings

I love to hate the Leafs; partly because I have 3 friends who support them so I like to wind them up. Partly because the Leafs seem like the Manchester United of the hockey world - fans all over the place!!

Joan Chisholm
Washington, England
Edmonton Oilers

As a Florida Panthers fan, I love to hate the Tampa Bay Lightning! I also hate the Red Wings, always have, and strong dislike of Jets. I do not like the way the owners moved the Thrashers and treated their fans after they paid for their season tickets and I am glad they didn't make the playoffs. I'm getting to not like the Penguins because they are 'cocky'; nobody has a divine right to make the playoffs and win everything and the team has more players than Crosby and Malkin.

Rebecca Hindle
Manchester, England
Florida Panthers

There's two I cannot stand for the life of me, the Anaheim Ducks for rivalry reasons, that and I also share my birthday with Ryan Getzlaf (May 10th) AND share my nickname with his son (albeit spelled differently, my Rider as opposed to his son's name being Ryder). Not to mention them winning the Cup in 2007 has left me a very bitter fan with revenge in mind. The other team I can't stand is the Canadiens. I think a part of me will forever rage due to the infamous moment that resulted in "Marty McSorely's Curse" and cost us the Cup, I'll die happily when we win enough

Ice Hockey Nights in Europe

Cups to give the Ducks the middle finger.

Kenny Jones
Caernarfon, Wales
LA Kings

Which teams do I love to hate? I don't hate any team. I have a strong dislike for the Ducks, like most Kings fans. I think their style of play is too far towards 'cheapshotting' and being physical in a dirty manner. I don't care much for the Canucks either, but that's because they don't play the game like real men, more like diving European footballers. Yes Alex Burrows, I'm looking at you. Teams in the East? Meh, West is best.

Stuart Coles
Coventry, England
LA Kings

The teams that I love to hate are the Detroit Red Wings and Los Angeles Kings. Detroit - my dislike grew for them because when I started getting into the NHL they always seemed to win. My fiancé calls this the 'Manchester United' syndrome. I also don't appreciate the Octopus thing they have going and I think that the jersey and logo is one of the most boring in the league. Los Angeles - I have a soft spot for the Ducks because of the Disney films and because Ryan Geztlaf plays for them. Because of this, I automatically started hating on the Kings. Rather randomly I have seen them live twice though, so I have had great fun rooting against them. Their logo, in all of its manifestations, is also boring.

Vicki Morgan
Basingstoke, England
Minnesota Wild

Boston Bruins. Where to start with reasons to hate this team? There are so many! Let's start with the very first thing you notice about them - the uniform. It's black and yellow, basically a bunch of men skating around an NHL ice rink dressed as bumble bees. It's unfortunate for their opponents, however, that these big bumble bees just happen to be oversized monsters on skates, more beasts than bees. They're the big bullies of the NHL world, a team that if they get a few goals up will just forget about playing hockey and beat you up instead. This is exactly what they did to Montreal in the 2010-11 season. At home with a handsome lead, they decided to start an all-out war on the ice which sure was fun to watch, old time hockey if you will, but didn't end nicely for my Habs either on the scoreboard or the treatment room. This was one of the main reasons I have grown to detest the Bruins, I never particularly liked them, playing a team six times a season and usually in the playoffs tends to have that effect. My hatred started in this match. It was brutal; the carnage was such that the goalies, Timmy Thomas and Carey Price, squared off and dropped the gloves. To compound matters, when the teams faced each other again the following month, the man who epitomised everything nasty about the Bruins, giant captain Zdeno Chara delivered a hit so devastating into the board/stanchion that it cracked Max Pacioretty's neck. Many a debate has been had over whether this was a deliberate act to injure the player, given the pair's history, any Habs fan will tell you what they think the answer to that debate to be. Later on that year, the Bruins knocked the Canadiens out of the playoffs in seven thrilling games to go and lift the cup. Rough justice for Habs fans. In a rivalry with a rich history, it was one that had just begun for me.

Chris Roderick
Ammanford, Wales
Montreal Canadiens

This is a pretty easy answer for me and probably for all Habs fans. Toronto Maple Leafs and Boston Bruins. Both are conference rivals, both teams don't like us in return and the games we play against each other are always huge occasions and entertaining games. Despite their lack of success recently, much to Montreal fans amusement, Toronto has always been huge rivals of ours. Due to the geographical situations of the two teams, the main languages spoken in the regions, the five Stanley Cup Finals we have played against each other; Habs fans are brought up not to like Maple Leaf fans and vice versa, it is engrained into the culture of the teams and fan bases. The Boston rivalry is known as one of the greatest rivalries in sport and although it has been going on for decades in recent years it has come to the boil and spilt over on several occasions. Since becoming a Montreal fan I have watched and 8-6 loss which involved two all-star goaltenders fighting in centre ice, a 7 game playoff series which ended in overtime heartache and the Bruins lifting the Stanley Cup. I love watching games against these two teams especially playoff games, not that Toronto gets many of them.... They are full of heart and passion, grit and determination. The feeling you get when beating these teams can't be matched by any other (non-playoff) game, neither can the disappointment if you lose against them.

Daniel Betts
Coventry, England
Montreal Canadiens

Ice Hockey Nights in Europe

Here is a list of teams I despise: Boston Bruins - being a Habs fan this is obvious, Chara just annoys me. Ottawa Senators - don't really have a reason beside them being in the North-East Division. Florida, Phoenix, Columbus- I don't like these teams as I feel that more teams should be in Canada and not in places where nobody cares about hockey.

Diarmuid Murray
Dublin, Rep of Ireland
Montreal Canadiens

I have a couple of teams for this. It used to be the Red Wings when I was growing up, but I can now actually sit through a Red Wings game and not feel the urge to throw objects at the TV. I now get the urge to do that with the Penguins and the Canucks. For some reason, the Penguins have this effect on commentators, whether they are Pens homers or not, that the Penguins can't do anything wrong and they are the greatest team under the sun. They have talented players but they are just one of those teams that get under my skin. With Canucks it's a bit different. The team is incredibly over-rated and their players don't do themselves any favours by letting go of dumb remarks and childish actions. Also, I think Canucks have some of the most annoying fans in the NHL. For example, the riots and the fact that the Canucks never seem to do anything wrong and their team is always hard done by.

Janne Virtanen
Hameenlinna, Finland (now Basingstoke, England)
Montreal Canadiens

Like most Devils fans, my hatred is firmly pointed towards the New York Rangers and the Philadelphia Flyers. I have been to a game at home for both the Flyers and the Rangers and also a road game in Philly. It felt amazing to join in with our Devils celebration chant of 'HEY YOU SUCK!' both times as well as our usual chant of 'RANGERS SUCK, FLYERS SWALLOW'. The Rangers are always such a dirty team, especially when playing us. A prime example of how much the teams hate each other was the game on 19th March 2012 at Madison Square Garden. As soon as the puck dropped for the start of the 1st period, 3 pairs of gloves hit the ice and fights broke out. The fans loved it! Philadelphia's game when I went over to the States was nerve racking.
There were a few times where I feared for my life, it sounds harsh but some people's definition of a bit of harmless fun may differ to mine. I felt so outnumbered; there I was, on my own in enemy territory, wearing a Devils

jersey with a British accent. The only positive I had on my side was that I am 6 feet 3 inches tall! The game was great though, although the Devils lost, it was an amazing experience.

Andreas Tatt
Bristol, England
New Jersey Devils

First of all the Rangers of course! Being a Devils fan, it is obvious that I hate the Rags.... and I surely don't need to explain the reason why. Also, the Penguins and for two different reasons: the first reason is that I really can't stand Sidney Crosby. To be honest it's not the player himself as I don't know him personally. It's the fact that it seems that, to the entire ice hockey world, he is ice hockey. He is a good player, one of the best, but not THE BEST. There are a bunch of players who are at his same level (or even better than him). To be honest, I was sorry he lost so many games because of the concussion, but can please someone explain me why "concussion" seemed to become a real matter only after Sidney's one? And what about all the players forced to retire because of concussion?
The second reason is James Neal: you could be right and there are only 12 Devils fans in the world, but please note that it's not the quantity but the quality that counts! Last but not least the Flyers. And in this case there is not a real reason why, I think I've never liked their jersey....

Emanuela Pozzi
Cernusco sul Naviglio, Italy
New Jersey Devils

Well for me this is an easy question! Being a Devils fan you quickly learn to hate the Rags and the Flyers, over the years with these teams we have built up some of the fiercest rivalries in hockey, most notably for me Stevens hit on Lindros with the Flyers and I feel after the triple fight incident off the opening face-off Devils Rags rivalry is at an all time high!

Gavin Clarke
Bristol, England
New Jersey Devils

It's New York Rangers! I'm big fan of New Jersey Devils, so it's understandable - rivalry. Big rivalry. I never liked Sean Avery, because he hates Marty Brodeur, one of my favourite players! Every game with Rangers is very emotional on and off the ice, Rangers hate Devils and Devils hate Rangers.

Ice Hockey Nights in Europe

So that's the reason, why I hate Rangers!

Michal Belšán
Chomutov, Czech Republic
New Jersey Devils

Even though I'm a newbie fan it didn't take me long to understand that I do hate the New York Rangers and the 'Filthy' Flyers!!

Orri Smarason
Reykjavík, Iceland
New Jersey Devils

As an Islanders fan, the only team I truly hate is the New York Rangers, and do I really need to explain why?

James Cartwright
Cardiff, Wales
New York Islanders

As a fan of an Atlantic Division team, it has to be our division rivals the Pittsburgh Penguins, Philadelphia Flyers, New Jersey Devils and New York Islanders. The Atlantic may be the only division in the NHL where bad blood exists between all five teams, and while it's hard to appreciate the geographical element to some of those rivalries, there no doubting the on-ice 'unpleasantries'. Those are the teams you want to beat as a Rangers fan, the wins that bring the biggest satisfaction.

Alex Nunn
Romford, England
New York Rangers

As for the team I love to hate, I would say I have several. Firstly, being a Rangers fan, naturally I hate every other Atlantic Division team! I also don't like the other Original Six teams either. Guess it must be a historical thing but yeah I would say those are the teams that annoy me the most! Actually, you can add the Vancouver Canucks to that list as well!

Daruish Gorgirzadeh
Bournemouth, England
New York Rangers

Jonathan Northall

It's the New Jersey Devils. As a Rangers fan they are massive local rivals and the hatred seems to be reflected on the ice. As part of my 30th birthday present, my wife organized a trip to New York to watch the Giants, unfortunately the Rangers were on a road trip so she got tickets to watch the Devils v Blue Jackets. This was her first foray into the world of hockey and she loved it, she came home and adopted the Devils as her team. As a result, I watch a fair few of their games with her on Gamecenter. So after checking for my brother-in-law's Oilers result, the Devils are the next team I look for. The match ups are quite lively and we watch them at home and I can safely say, I hate losing too them.

Ed Johnston
Somerset, England
New York Rangers

Penguins, Flyers, Devils, Islanders. Of course, it's because they're all in the Atlantic Division too. I have a stern dislike for the Boston Bruins too. That probably stems from my NFL support, being a New York Jets fan and hating the New England Patriots.
At the end of the day, provided the Rangers win and their nearest rivals lose it's all good with me.

James Willis
Watford, England
New York Rangers

I think I love only one team, my favourite team: Ottawa Senators. I like Vancouver Canucks too, but this is different level than Sens. To be honest, I have to say I can't count any team which I hate because I think I don't hate any.
Of course, I have few teams which I dislike - but I will never call this 'hate'. On that list I have: Boston Bruins, Toronto Maple Leafs, Montreal Canadiens, Philadelphia Flyers.

Krzysztof Sankiewicz
Warsaw, Poland
Ottawa Senators

Only one team boils my blood: the Montreal Canadians. It's based on a nasty combination of smug superiority, based on days long gone by, snivelling insecurity and whining.
A team devoid of a back bone couldn't even muster enough 'balls' to have a crack at Chara. As for the 'Ole' chants, don't get me started. Montreal, you

Ice Hockey Nights in Europe

truly need to get over yourselves.

Rob Carter
Newcastle, England
Ottawa Senators

No surprises here, it's the Toronto Maple Leafs! Being a Sens fan comes hand in hand with disliking the Leafs and following fellow Senators fans on Twitter, many of them from Ontario, has allowed me an insight on why I should hate the Leafs and a taste of the rivalry between the two teams.

Robert Weaver
Gloucestershire, England
Ottawa Senators

We used to have a very strong rivalry with the New York Rangers back in the 1980's, but they are by far my least hated team in the Atlantic Division. I loathe the New Jersey Devils, simply because of their game. I appreciate that 'the trap' has been around for many years prior to the 1990's, but the Devils took this defensive strategy, mastered it, and slowed the game right down. Now, I cannot bear to watch them play. Funnily enough, I don't 'hate' the Penguins as much as most Flyers fans do. Of course, I don't like them, but I respect what Bylsma has done with the team bringing up AHL players, albeit through injuries, and competing successfully at an NHL level.

David Lidbury
Bristol, England
Philadelphia Flyers

Pittsburgh Penguins - State rival and prone to tanking to get good again. They've been blessed with great players like Jagr and Lemieux and then more recently Crosby and Malkin. All four were/are a joy to watch play, if you could ignore the emblem on the front of their jersey. Matt Cooke is not a likeable player. New York Rangers - The fact that they're are becoming a threat again and that they have had our number this year only makes it worse. Back in 2009, I went to a Flyers versus Rangers game at MSG and the amount of abuse from the Rangers fans to those of us in orange was more than expected. That being said, you don't mind, it's part of the atmosphere. 24/7 has helped me to appreciate the personalities of some of their players and even their coach. Other minor ones: Devils - not so much as before. They played a boring but effective style of game and Scott Stevens ruined Lindros. Red Wings - Was friends with an Avs fan at school. This was during their big rivalry. I took the Avs side, but you can't

Jonathan Northall

help but respect how the Wings have been this good for this long. Capitals - not so much hate, but I do like to see them struggle.

Ray Skeates
Basingstoke, England
Philadelphia Flyers

Just as in sports you have a team or player you root for, you also need a team or player to boo relentlessly. For me, that team is the cross-state rivals; the Pittsburgh Penguins. Not a huge fan, and the fact that it seems the league and media are all over Crosby and Malkin just adds fuel to the fire. Of course it's always nice when the Flyers beat them though! I'm not a fan of the Rangers or the Devils either, but not as much as the Penguins!

Tim Barnes
Cambridge, England (born in New Jersey, USA)
Philadelphia Flyers

Being a Coyotes fan, and the subsequent lack of any real success there are not many teams I love to hate. But there are two! Since arriving in Phoenix the Coyotes have had some forays into the postseason, but are yet to get past the first round. After the lockout and up to the current season the Coyotes have faced the Detroit Red Wings in two playoff series back to back. Both times, the Red Wings came out on top, winning the best of seven series in 2010 and sweeping the 'Yotes' in 2011. It is for this reason I despise them. The Red Wings are a stronger team, I don't think there is any Coyotes fan that will dispute that, but the Red Wings are the archetypal 'old NHL'. A founding member, Original Six, they have been around forever! The relentless money making machine has everything the Coyotes don't! The other thing I hate about them is their fans. Most have the air of authority about them, almost thinking, I'm a Wings fan so I'm instantly better than you are. Plus, maybe this is a symptom of Phoenix in general but, there are so many of them in Phoenix!!! They only ever come out when the Wings are in town! If they are such big hockey fans why the hell do they not come to more Coyotes games? The second team, are the newly formed Winnipeg Jets. Their detestation of the Coyotes is matched by my hatred of them! I think most Jets fans have finally got over the chip in their shoulder of having 'their' team taken away from them, but no city is guaranteed to keep its franchise, something I'm painfully aware of being a Coyotes fan.

Mark Woodcock
Macclesfield, England
Phoenix Coyotes

Ice Hockey Nights in Europe

Philadelphia for all the obvious reasons as a Pens fan, I don't think it needs explaining! I'm really not a fan of the Montreal Canadians. I hate how they seem to be the default team to support for many people in Britain when they decide to get into watching NHL hockey and I hate the way their fans believe they have some sort of entitlement to success just because of their history.

James Bird
Burnley, England
Pittsburgh Penguins

To be fair, I don't hate any other team really. I have a dislike for the Philadelphia Flyers, mainly due to the fact that they seem to be a bit of a mental block for the Pittsburgh Penguins. I always love to win against them.

Katrina Gordon
Glasgow, Scotland
Pittsburgh Penguins

You would have thought it would be simple to identify the one team that at their mere thought causes the bile to rise in your throat, your temples to pound and your fists to clench. Traditional rivalries going back over the years would be simple to call such as Pens/Flyers/Rangers from the days of the Atlantic Division. Some of those traditional rivalries have stayed the course whilst others have come and gone. The Battle of the Turnpike is still as important as ever to Penguins fans but different more personal rivalries have brought on intensity to games the Washington Capitals or Detroit Red Wings. So is it a team or a player that dictates the teams you love to hate? Mine would have to be a player. Wherever Sean Avery went, my hatred of the team was sure to follow. Deemed an agitator, he displayed a clear lack of respect for the game and the fans that paid his wages as well as his fellow professionals. His retirement created a void in my team hatred, but it's always good to reach back in time and pluck a memory like the toy found in a box in the garage.

Rob Aherne
Stafford, England
Pittsburgh Penguins

Jonathan Northall

Hate is a strong word and one that I don't use often. But I can honestly say, hand on heart, that I hate the Philadelphia Flyers. Why? Well I suppose it's expected of a Pens fan, but there's more to it than that. I do genuinely hate everything about them. Their players, I mean seriously, who doesn't hate Scott Hartnell? And then there's their jersey. I really, truly, hate it. So much so that the very sight of someone wearing it gets my heckles up. I hate their building, I hate their goal horn - everything, I just simply hate them. It's not just because I'm a Pens fan. For me, it's like knowing the difference between right and wrong. Good and evil. It's essentially instinctive, almost a natural, unprompted response to anything to do with their horrible team. I don't pretend to hate them because I should do; it's a genuine hatred of everything they stand for. Some years ago, we were driving back to New York from Atlanta and drove through Philadelphia. Merely being there had a strange effect on me. In fact I had to try really hard to stop myself from winding the window down to spit on the road we were driving on. It was making my skin creep. And to be fair that's probably about it. Although, it would remiss of me if I didn't mention the Devils and the Habs....

Rob Howe
Sheffield, England
Pittsburgh Penguins

As a lifelong Pittsburgh Penguins fan there are two teams that I absolutely despise: the Philadelphia Flyers and Boston Bruins. Having lived in L.A. throughout my 20's & 30's I also need to add the worst NHL fan base ever to this list: the San Jose Sharks. Having moved to Philadelphia after my parents' divorce and having a Flyers season ticket holder as a stepfather I was "fortunate" to have attended countless games at the old Spectrum in South Philly. I can tell you this: ALL the rumours you have heard about Flyers fans are 100% true! They are the rudest, crudest most Neanderthal-like fans in the league. They will not hesitate to smack a little kid (even a girl) in the back of the head if they wear a visiting teams colours, and the constant jabs at Sidney Crosby (and decades earlier at Mario Lemieux) for being a "wuss" are completely mystifying to me. Boston Bruins fans, on the other hand, simply are annoying since they whine and complain so much. I first recall my disdain for them during halftime of Super Bowl XIV. While my Pittsburgh Steelers were on their way to winning their fourth NFL Championship in just six years, the Penguins had a live press conference to announce they were changing their colours from blue & white to black & gold to match that of the Steelers and current baseball World Champion Pittsburgh Pirates. The Bruins immediately cried foul and demanded the NHL to disallow the Penguins from "stealing their colours". The league overruled this since Pittsburgh had an NHL team before the Bruins existed

Ice Hockey Nights in Europe

(the Pirates of 1925-30) and they used black & gold first. In the early '90's when the Pens twice beat the B's in the playoffs on their way to the Stanley Cup, Boston coach Mike Milbury again started to moan and groan over the Penguins and Swedish tough guy Ulf Samuelsson "playing dirty"....simply because he knew how to hit hard! Having adopted the Los Angeles Kings as my "2nd favourite team" during my 14 years in California, I quickly adopted disrespect for their arch rivals the San Jose Sharks. Not only did the Sharks steal the Penguins patented "shark chomp" and Jaws theme music used during the 1991 and 1992 Cup runs, their fans to this day never seemed to learn the rules of hockey. I lived in San Francisco for three years after L.A. and went to many Sharks game in nearby S.J. The crowd mostly consists of Silicon Valley yuppies who only attend games at H.P. Pavilion since Google, Apple, eBay, YouTube, etc. have corporate season tickets there. Go to any game at "The Shark Tank" and you will be guaranteed to hear phrases such as "What is icing?", "When does the fourth quarter start?" and the best one "What does the 'C' on that guy's jersey mean?" Hard to believe that after 20 years people in the Bay Area still don't understand this great sport!

Robert Campbell
Pittsburgh, USA (now Uppsala, Sweden)
Pittsburgh Penguins

As a Penguins fan, I think it comes natural to hate or not like Philadelphia Flyers, Washington Capitals and Detroit Red Wings. Flyers are obviously a Divisional rival and they come from the same State. And they wear orange. That's my least favourite colour. Washington Capitals have Alex Ovechkin, who claims to be better than Penguins superstar Crosby. I can't forget the fact one of their players injured Sidney Crosby. When it comes to Detroit Red Wings, I think is just the 2008 and 2009 Stanley Cup Finals. I also don't like teams like Phoenix Coyotes, Florida Panthers, Tampa Bay Lightning, LA Kings, San Jose Sharks, Anaheim Ducks...hockey is supposed to be winter sport and they don't have it, that's the only reason.

Sanja Prošek
Ljubljana, Slovenia
Pittsburgh Penguins

I HATE the Flyers. I hate their history and everything the franchise is built on. I hate their puke orange jerseys. I hate Bobby Clarke and his stick swinging, ankle breaking antics and toothless grin. I hate that Talbot now plays for them. I hate when they are able to beat the Penguins. I hate their obnoxious fans when they are winning, and whining when they are losing. I

Jonathan Northall

hate those 80's Cooperall pants.

Stephen Butler
Leicester, England
Pittsburgh Penguins

Since I've followed the NHL, I've probably hated every team the Penguins have played against at one time or another, but the teams I love to hate the most are the Philadelphia Flyers, Washington Capitals and the Montreal Canadiens. The Flyers and Capitals have a huge rivalry with the Penguins, making the games even better to watch. To see the fans of those teams show so much hatred towards us makes you want to beat them that little bit more. To beat both those teams on the way to the cup in 2009 made winning the Stanley Cup that little bit sweeter. My reason for not liking the Montreal Canadiens is I simply just can't stand their fans and how they constantly boo every time something isn't going their way! Losing to them in the 2010 playoffs was a hard one to take.

Tom Harding
Isle of Wight, England
Pittsburgh Penguins

Well, I really don't hate any team, because hate is a really harsh word. That said I do hate the Flyers and the Senators as much as I can hate any team in the greatest game in the world. Their style of play has always been one you loved to hate and one you loved watching if your team was playing it. Hard fought series, player rivalries is what makes those games special for players and fans alike.

Mislav Jantoljak
Zagreb, Croatia
Pittsburgh Penguins / Toronto Maple Leafs

Easy – "DUCKS SUCK!!! DUCKS SUCK!!! DUCKS SUCK!!!" (The famous chant outside, whilst we queue up to get into HP Pavilion, and then inside when we beat up on them on the ice). GO SHARKS!!! Not too keen on Dallas Stars (Divisional rivals), Detroit Red Wings (Playoff rivals), Chicago Blackhawks and Vancouver Canucks either thanks to painful playoff losses.

Jason Dunn
Woking, England
San Jose Sharks

Ice Hockey Nights in Europe

First up, our hated rivals, the Detroit Red Wings and the Chicago Blackhawks. Two classless teams with terrible fans, acting entitled in the case of Detroit and 'bandwagonners' in the case of Chicago. Both teams make cheap shots and seemingly get favourable calls. Other teams include Boston, as I'm a part-time Canucks fan too. The sheer nastiness of that side and the arrogance in which they strut around the ice and foul with impunity fills me with rage. Brad Marchand is one of my most hated players. Finally, the Winnipeg Jets. This is purely because of the fans. I used to have a soft spot for Atlanta, they had a horrific management structure and ownership, but I liked the passion of the fans and the honesty of some of the players. Then came the move to Winnipeg and their fans were so classless, instead of acknowledging the Atlanta fans and acting with humility, they swamped various Atlanta blogs and such with gloating comments and 'you have no fans' chants. A really horrible thing to do and it turned me off the franchise forever.

Grant Sales
High Wycombe, England
St Louis Blues

As with most St Louis Blues fans, I can list all our division rivals as hated teams – the Red Wings and Blackhawks most especially. There's a level of hatred for them that's difficult to define. Saying that, I do have friends who are Red Wing fans. For me, personally, there are other teams/players I hate. First up, Joe Thornton – for the hit that put Perron out of the game for over a year and Thornton's disrespectful comments of "that guy" when referring to Perron afterwards. As a result of this, I loathe the entire Sharks team – and it was wonderfully poetic that we beat them in round 1 of the playoffs. The Anaheim Ducks are another hated team. The first time I watched the Blues play live and in the flesh was in Anaheim against the Ducks. We had seats only a couple of rows from the glass. Ryan Getzlaf got away with a blatant "knee on knee" on Barret Jackman – the ref ignored it completely. Jackman was down on the ice – and typically the Ducks scored. The Canucks are another team – for the total lack of respect for anyone else.

Sandra Pascoe
Penzance, England
St Louis Blues

Jonathan Northall

I don't really have a dislike for any teams in general, as long as I get to see a good game, but if I had to pick a couple of teams it would the Flyers and Blackhawks as the friends that watch our local team support them!!

Alan Giles
Reading, England
Tampa Bay Lightning

Even though I'm not a person that would enjoy hating on somebody I have to admit there are indeed teams I can't talk about without feeling a bit of an anger or some bitterness in my mouth. At the very top (or at the lowest point if you'd like) are the Pittsburgh Penguins. I don't like them, at all. If I was to use one word to describe them I'd say "arrogant". Also, I have yet to find a Penguins fan who I could lead a normal, constructive discussion with. I don't want to generalize anyone, I'm sure there must be some good fans amongst the Pens fandom, I just haven't met them yet. Same goes to the other team that causes my stomach to flip – Boston Bruins. Besides arrogant, I'd add a word "dirty". And that's all I'm gonna say about this topic because it wouldn't be wise to continue. I might say things I would regret in the end....

Katerina Brzonova
Zlin, Czech Republic
Tampa Bay Lightning

I have to start with our instate rivals the Florida Panthers, just because, they are like a pesky younger brother who won't leave you alone. Next has to be the Boston Bruins, a big rivalry with the amount of fans they have in the Tampa area, they take over our arena, are loud, obnoxious, and currently have Milan Lucic. Knocking us out of the Conference finals made things worse too. Have to also include the Habs for their constant thought that it's their divine right to have Vinny Lecavalier on their team. And, lastly, anyone who Matt Cooke is currently playing for.

Nathan Cartmel
Bristol, England (now Tampa, FL, USA)
Tampa Bay Lightning

Being a Leafs fan, there are the obvious few teams such as Montreal, and Ottawa that we all have our disagreements with, but the two teams that I love to hate are Detroit and New York Rangers. The Red Wings is probably more of a fevered rivalry rather than hatred simply because of the magnificent history we share going all the way back to Stanley Cup finals way back when, right up to that incredible 7 game 1st round series in '93, but nevertheless it still makes me smile when they lose!

As for the Rangers, I think it stems from the sense of self-importance the Rangers give themselves. They think the world owes them something just because they are from the Big Apple, which is strange because you don't get that same feeling with the Islanders. The Rangers and their fans deep-down believe that the league couldn't survive without them and that they are doing us all a favour by being here, and that they have some God given right to win every game every year.

Christopher Barr
Dungannon, Northern Ireland
Toronto Maple Leafs

Definitely, Philadelphia Flyers. Don't know why, they are just despised.

Elliott Hall
Sheffield, England
Toronto Maple Leafs

Montreal Canadiens – It's a Leafs tradition, so it goes without saying. Ottawa Senators - Pretty much as above - there have been some cracking (although sadly, some dull) "Battles of Ontario" over the years. Victory over either of the above tastes sweeter than any other team.

Gord Turner
Manchester, England
Toronto Maple Leafs

As a Leafs fan from England, I hate the Montreal Canadiens! Adding the NHL rivalry between the Leafs and the Habs to the Anglo-French rivalry in an Englishman's blood, means I really can't stand them!

I hate their arrogant attitude, thinking they're the best NHL team of all time. Their Anglophobe attitude, as demonstrated by protesting because their coach couldn't speak French. All of which makes every win against them so special, but also makes the defeats that much harder to take, especially the one I attended in 2009, a few days after the Leafs annual elimination from the post-season play-off chase, meaning there was a large number of Habs fans in attendance at the Air Canada Centre to see them beat us 6-2.

Jonathan Northall

I was gutted. Devastated. That memory makes every late night win on TV back home very enjoyable! Go Leafs!

Jamie Mash
Northallerton, England
Toronto Maple Leafs

Being a Leaf fan, our most hated rivals will always be the Montreal Canadiens due the proximity and history between the two teams. In more recent times, the Boston Bruins have been the team I love to hate. They have our number, especially in this 2011/2012 season and Tim Thomas in net seems to be able to make saves with his eyes shut. Their fans love to taunt Phil Kessel after we traded for him. Their captain Zdeno Chara, a monster at 6ft 9in, uses his size to intimidate players but will only fight lightweights and there is the infamous Pacioretty incident as well.

Mark Rackham
Kent, England
Toronto Maple Leafs

I don't really hate any teams; I've never understood that base mentality of liking one team meaning you have to hate another. That said, as a Leafs fan the Senators and the Habs are our pantomime villains, generally one of them is worse than us at any given time, which gives us something to feel a little better about when we're languishing in the lower depths of the conference. In the couple of years I've been watching closely I've grown to dislike the Bruins too, not the fans or the organisation, but the current line-up and the way they play... I like hard physical hockey, but they all too often cross the line into downright dirty play. It doesn't make me angry but it's disappointing and I guess in the end that's worse!

Matt Merritt
Portsmouth, England
Toronto Maple Leafs

As a Leafs fan it has to be the Senators or the Canadiens, they are the obvious ones, but I also have a healthy hatred for the Bruins. I always think of what could have been if we hadn't made the worst trades possible to the Bruins, in Kessel and Rask. One day we'll have our way, one day.

Richard Trowbridge
Cheltenham, England
Toronto Maple Leafs

Ice Hockey Nights in Europe

As a Maple Leafs fan the easy answer to this would be the Senators, or Canadiens. However, I don't hate either of them. In fact, I don't hate any team in the NHL (no, not even the Canucks). Part of the reason I follow the NHL is that what I actually hate (and to a certain extent don't understand) is the tribalism that surrounds supporting a team in the domestic UK football leagues. If I were an Arsenal supporter I would be expected to hate Tottenham Hotspur, for no obvious reason that I can make out. Following the NHL gives me a disconnection from being brought up to hate another team. There are parts of every single NHL team that I admire (even Columbus) and would much prefer to for that than ignore them simply because I'm meant to hate them.

Tom Mannington
London, England
Toronto Maple Leafs

Overall, it has to be the Habs, Montreal Canadiens, due to the traditional rivalry with the Leafs down the years. Although, after watching games this season, I have to admit to disliking the Ottawa Senators even more as those games have seemed more intense due to the fan rivalry and the games have been much more physical.

Tony Harrison
Rutland, England
Toronto Maple Leafs

Team I love to hate: New York Rangers: the coach, the players, especially Lundqvist and Gaborik. Gaborik is easy: his dirty hit from behind, on Islanders Frans Nielsen, near the end of regular season in 2010/2011. The hit gave Nielsen concussion-like symptoms, and kept him from playing for the Danish national team at the World Championships. As the Danish national hockey team had been struggling to stay on top, this was a big hit for us especially since the player himself really wanted to play. Gaborik only got a two minute boarding penalty for it, but I will dislike him for the rest of his active years.

Kristina Stryhn Laursen
Copenhagen, Denmark
Toronto Maple Leafs / New York Islanders

Being still quite new to the sport I'm still becoming familiar with the hockey rivalries. As a Canucks fan I'm adopting the teams rivalries with Chicago

Jonathan Northall

and Boston and learning to love to hate them. I think in the last few years with the Canucks adopting the Northwest Division I'm not really bothered about the Divisional rivalries. They are always enjoyable to watch but not as frustrating as a loss to a team such as Chicago after our many Playoff rivalries.

Dan Birkin
Burton upon Trent, England
Vancouver Canucks

As a Canucks fan I couldn't despise the Bruins much more. It's not just sour chops from the Stanley Cup, no. My blood curdles at the sight of some of their players. They are a team that takes malicious hits to the extreme; I think they feel willing to do anything to irritate the opposition because their captain Zdeno 'Giant' Chara has got their backs. The main protagonist is Brad Marchand, many of my friends know my description of him is not suitable for public ears, let's just say the boy is a weasel who should concentrate on being more stealthy in his movement than trying to hand out concussions. The other team I just have a personal loathing for is Minnesota, and I don't even know why. They're not a threat to my team, they don't have a huge physical presence on the ice and they have never hurt one of my boys. I have no idea why but I really don't like watching them, hearing about them or seeing their awful green and cream jerseys.

Joanne Turner
Leeds, England
Vancouver Canucks

I don't think I love to hate a team. It's either love or hate! On the other hand, most NHL teams are neutral to me. I tend to dislike teams that play a certain way or have a certain quality. I really disliked the pre-lockout Toronto Maple Leafs, always rich, always willing to overpay a player - plus they played nasty all too often. Nowadays I'm not a fan of Boston Bruins, for the obvious reasons and for the fact that I actually followed the Bruins that year and cheered for the Canucks-Bruins final. It turned me sour. Sometimes you dislike a team because of certain players. I hate players with big egos who did not prove much yet. Los Angeles Kings are a good example. They were neutral to me a couple of years ago, but the arrogant duo of Drew Doughty and Jack Johnson did the trick. I don't like that team at all now and it has absolutely nothing to do with current playoffs. I want to add that if a team changes its culture or rebuilds, I stop disliking them. Example: I have nothing against the Leafs now, I also admire how nice

Colorado is rebuilding – didn't really like them pre-lockout.

Michał Pręgowski
Warsaw, Poland
Vancouver Canucks

Pittsburgh Penguins: It started with my dislike of Sidney Crosby and has just grown from there. The NHL have tried to create a rivalry between Crosby and Ovechkin which led to Crosby/Pens fans and particularly the Canadian and Pittsburgh media constantly criticising Ovechkin and getting digs in which hurt me because nobody wants to see their favourite player getting criticised. This pretty much started my dislike of them and it's just got stronger and stronger each year.

Hana Imiolczyk
Merthyr Tydfil, Wales
Washington Capitals

Obviously, the Pittsburgh Penguins, just the whole rivalry thing, and they have recently won the trophy that the Caps strive for. I'm not a fan of the Philly Flyers, I don't like their style of play, unnecessarily aggressive, but I suppose it works for them.

Nick Gresty
Manchester, England
Washington Capitals

The team I really can't stand is the New York Rangers. I absolutely hate them. I don't even know why, probably because they are so darn good and arrogant because of that. And HBO's 24/7 obviously didn't help, since my second team is Philadelphia. Especially great deal of hate I hold for their ex-coach John Tortorella, I couldn't be in the same room with that guy, not for a minute. Because my second team is Philadelphia, I have some serious issues with the Penguins. Especially after this last game that Philly won, their fans are… wrong, to say the least.

Štěpánka Černá
Dolní Němčí, Czech Republic
Winnipeg Jets

Jonathan Northall

4 WHO ARE YOUR FAVOURITE PLAYERS AND WHY?

After the negativity of the last chapter, I offer a positive chapter to glorify the personal heroes of European fans. On reflection, there were three tranches of choice: universally accepted players, team heroes and unsung heroes. Firstly, iconic names such as Howe, Orr, Lemieux and Gretzky litter the submission with enormous regularity. I think this highlights how much European fans are students of the game. Secondly, it is team heroes who are celebrated by fans. These are players that have an iconic status with their team but maybe don't have the same recognition at the first group. Finally, we have the unsung heroes. Players that many fans will say "who?"

Like most I like the likes of Mark Messier, Gordie Howe, Wayne Gretzky, Mario Lemieux however the players I really admire are the likes of the 4th line scrubs who work their butts off to protect their spot on the roster and don't take things for granted...as such one of my favourite players in recent years is the late Rick Rypien. He played for the Canucks and signed with the Jets in the summer of 2011 but sadly would never play for them. He suffered some set backs with injuries on a few occasions one of which was serious, not once did he think his roster spot was safe unlike what some other NHL'ers might think is their God given right. Rypien had to work tooth and nail to get back into shape and heal from surgery and fight for his roster spot, thus earning the respect of management, teammates and fans alike. We now know this was even tougher for Rick as it became aware since his passing that he had suffered from severe depression. Coming back time and time again from injury is one thing but to suffer from depression is a huge testament to him. He suffered from some bad times in his life with a very close friend being tragically killed in a car crash. Rick was a gutsy guy on the ice with his work ethic; he was an even better person off the ice, as most tough guys tend to be. My other favourite player is recently retired Darcy Tucker, he played with an edge, heart, soul, passion and with a spark, he would never give up hope especially if the Leafs were losing. He would be a motivator to the team and the fans time and time again to turn things around. Tucker would take a hit to give a hit and get under the oppositions skin especially when he took on the entire Ottawa bench.

AJ
Not disclosed
Toronto Maple Leafs

Ice Hockey Nights in Europe

For me its Martin St. Louis, the guy is pretty much an ever present on the team sheet, and he just produces season in and out, and for a guy that went undrafted and was deemed too short to play at the highest level is no mean feat. He gets players to produce around him too, he has helped Stamkos and others reach another level.

Alan Giles
Reading, England
Tampa Bay Lightning

For me, it's Henrik Lundqvist and Brendan Shanahan. While Shanahan's inconsistencies as the NHL's chief disciplinarian frustrate me to no end, he was always my favourite player on the ice. His commitment toward his teammates was perhaps the biggest factor for me, something epitomised by his fight with Donald Brashear in December 2006. He had character and heart, not to mention a tremendous scoring record, throughout his career in the NHL. I'm glad he had a chance to bring his game to Broadway before calling it a day. Lundqvist has been the backbone of the current Rangers roster for years now. Much like Shanahan, he has that steely determination and will to win that never seems to fade. He's a fighter, one that's had to carry this team through several mediocre campaigns with little offensive support. He'll continue to be the Rangers most important player until he hangs up his skates.

Alex Nunn
Romford, England
New York Rangers

I think there is no question about our favourite players: Marty St. Louis and Steven Stamkos. It's very impressive to see with how much enthusiasm St Louis plays the game and what he is able to bring on the table in spite of his age. He is not only a very good player but also an impressive person. One of his major tasks during the last few years was the co-teaching of SS91! We saw him the first time in 2008 with Marty during the World Cup in Switzerland. Despite of his talent he works hard, improves his place, especially defensively and you hear nothing like escapades from him!

Alexander, Daniela & Marek Neumann
Schwäbisch Hall, Germany
Tampa Bay Lightning

Jonathan Northall

I could probably spend several pages talking about my love for Teemu Selanne. I've seen him play since he was a junior at Jokerit, and in many ways he is the reason I am a hockey fan. He not only defines the Ducks as a franchise. He also, for me, is everything a hockey player should be: humble, honest and undyingly committed. He has realised that, unlike other sports, it has to be a team effort. No one is bigger than the sum of the team's parts. He makes me smile every time he skates – as you know he is playing the game he loves, and wants people to enjoy what he does. The definition of an All-Star. In terms of others, Jiggy (Giguere) will always hold a special place for me for how he put the team on his back, and carried them through the playoffs (twice). Outside of the Ducks, probably my all time favourite player is Eric Lindros. I idolised the power of his play growing up, and I just loved the way the LOD line played hockey. Power, speed and incredible skill. I also loved Dominic Hasek – he defined a new way of goaltending, and the perfect antidote for the unnerving boring brilliance of watching Brodeur play!

Allan Allison
Bristol, England
Anaheim Ducks

Tim Thomas - because he never give up on the puck and is the first to admit it if he made a mistake. Bobby Orr - for that classic goal celebration after scoring the winning Stanley Cup goal. Marian Gaborik - because the goals he scores are amazing.

Amy Hill
Camberley, England
Boston Bruins

Since I have only been really serious about my hockey for just over a year now, most of my favourites are pretty current NHL players. I have a particular fondness for the younger players of the games because I will be able to follow the ups and downs of their hopefully long careers. Jordan Eberle and Tyler Seguin are two players who stand out to me for their respective talents within the game. Most of the young Oilers with Nugent-Hopkins and Hall are also among my notable interests. Apart from this, my favourite absolute player is one who was cruelly taken out of the game around the time I started watching, and is unlikely to ever play again: Marc Savard. Because of this, I hold him in high esteem for his raw talent and because we will never see him shine on the ice again. Looking over the history of my chosen teams the great ones of the 1970's Bruins are prevalent: Orr, Esposito and Sanderson. It is difficult for me to look back in the past at the teams solely because I was not around to watch them play, to grow up with them.

Andrew Best
Bracknell, England
Boston Bruins

From the past, Peter Forsberg was just amazing. Great hands, super speed, strong, a great leader and down to earth. It's such a shame his career was ruined by injuries, if he was healthy, he could have been one of the best of all time. These days, I love the speed of Giroux at the Flyers and Milan Lukic at Boston. He is a super power forward and was outstanding in the 2011 success.

Andy Parsons
London, England
Colorado Avalanche

I love Shawn Thornton! Always able to mobilize other Bruins the good fight always defends the other Bruins players. I like his aggressive style of play. Oh...and Milan Lucic for the same reasons

Bartek Pexu
Warsaw, Poland
Boston Bruins

My favourite all time player is Steve Yzerman, he was the first player to be an idol to me and is arguably the best player Detroit have ever had. However, Nik Lidstrom is right up there with him. For me, he is the ultimate idol for fans of the sport. He has conducted himself perfectly across his entire career and will deserve his instant entry into the Hall of Fame. A bit of a curve ball from me now though, my current favourite on the roster (aside from Lidstrom) is Darren Helm, he is so under-rated, but he works so hard that he allows the stars to shine. His importance was proved in the end of the season, when injury forced him out and the team suffered badly as a result. He may never be a Hall of Famer, but real fans will remember how important he is in keeping the team competitive.

Bradley Marsh
Essex, England
Detroit Red Wings

Jonathan Northall

I think my favourite player from the past is Cam Neely. He was gritty and I loved watching the way he hit people when he was playing the puck. My favourite player from the present team is Patrice Bergeron who seems to be the one player to consistently be in the right place at the right time and feeds the puck to the right place on the ice every time. He really is the most underrated player in the NHL today in my opinion.

Callum Sweeting
Hull, England
Boston Bruins

My favourite player in the whole game has to be Ryan Callahan. He plays the game with such heart, grit and determination and he is a brilliant leader. Here is a list of my other favourite players for other reasons: Henrik Lundqvist - best goaltender in the NHL at the moment and genuinely nice guy. The whole NY Rangers team - watching HBO 24/7 was a great insight into their team chemistry and what makes them tick! The two that stood out were Brandon Prust and Brian Boyle. They were hilarious as a double act! Claude Giroux - great player and a likeable guy off the ice too, even if he is a Flyers player. Evgeni Malkin - best player in the league, great to watch. Jonathan Toews and Patrick Kane - two unbelievable talents and around for a long time! Steven Stamkos - pure sniper and an absolute beast!

Daruish Gorgirzadeh
Bournemouth, England
New York Rangers

If you know me, you will know that I am a huge fan of Simon Gagne. He is by far my favourite player to play in the NHL. My admiration for left-winger Simon Gagne did not come until he lit the lamp with an overtime GWG in Game 6 of the 2004 Conference Finals against the Tampa Bay Lightning. I fully appreciate Gagne's game and how he can be used in all-situations, utilizing his blazing speed to create breakaways. He was, and still is, a fan favourite in Philadelphia and I was very sad to see him leave first time around. I have personally not met Simon but he seems to be as good off the ice as he is on it. Since 2000, he has adopted an annual golf tournament in his hometown (Ste. Foy, Quebec) to raise money to benefit kids with leukaemia.

David Lidbury
Bristol, England
Philadelphia Flyers

The top one is Joe Sakic. He was born to be leader on and also off the ice. The current Avalanche squad is missing this kind of player. The result? They missed playoffs for the third time over the last four years. Every team would be successful with Sakic. Do not forget he was not only leader with "C" on his chest. He was also great scorer and led all players in many statistics. He retired and everything has changed. I have also other favourite players, but they are very far away behind "Super Joe". Patrick Roy is the best goaltender in the history of hockey, Adam Foote was the classic kind of defensive defenseman, Matt Duchene should be the next all-star player and Gabriel Landeskog is another young element on the roster.

David Púchovský
Bratislava, Slovakia
Colorado Avalanche

I'm not really a guy who focuses on single players; team effort should always come first. Right now my favourite is probably Christian Ehrhoff because he is a defender who is exciting to watch on offense while still playing a reliable game in his own zone and standing up for his goalie. He fought multiple times this year to protect his goalie even though he isn't a fighter at all. Ryan Miller, Tyler Myers and Jason Pominville are coming in next. Marcus Foligno and Tyler Ennis are on a good way to become favourites as well, but aren't established enough yet. There are some more guys around the league that I like, but I don't see them nearly enough to make a well-informed statement on them.

David Trippler
Mainz, Germany
Buffalo Sabres

Many players I like from down the years but here is a list of my favourites: Wayne Gretzky - synonymous with ice-hockey, magnificent player, leading the Edmonton Oilers to 4 of their 5 Stanley Cups and truly deserves the moniker of "The Great One". Maurice "The Rocket" Richard - the player that inarguably means the most to the Montreal Canadiens, a winner of several Stanley Cups and the first person to score 50 goals in one season Mario Lemieux - brilliantly talented player, portrayed magnificent skills on the ice and is now the Owner of the Pittsburgh Penguins, I have so much respect for this man due to his work in preserving the Penguins' Legacy. Jean Béliveau - the most successful player ever in Montreal Canadiens and NHL history, being part of 17 Stanley Cup winning teams (10 as a player, 7 as staff). Jean, along with The Rocket, is the player that means the most to the Habs fans. Bobby Orr - it would be impossible to list great NHL players without mentioning quite possibly the best Defenceman to ever play the game, there is a reason why he is one of Don Cherry's favourite players simply because he was that damn good. Patrick Roy - legendary goalie for Montreal and Colorado. Jacques Plante - mainly due to his contributions towards usage of goalie masks. Guy Lafleur - "The Flower" is one of my favourite players, the top scoring Habs player of all-time and a great talent on the ice. Sidney Crosby - one of the best hockey players I have seen and quite possibly the most important player currently in the NHL, "The Kid" has all the talent to become one of the greats. Nicklas Lidström - my favourite defenceman who is currently active, Lidstrom will be a player held in the same regard as Bobby Orr due to his success with the Red Wings.

Diarmuid Murray
Dublin, Rep of Ireland
Montreal Canadiens

Ryan Callahan is my favourite Rangers player. He's not the flashiest of players and he doesn't probably get the attention he deserves but he has such heart and grit. It's admirable stuff, as captain of the team, he is pretty much the heart beat. Gaborik will get you the goals, Richards has the silky skills and vision but Cally would be the first name on my team sheet. Outside of the Rangers I, like everyone else no doubt, enjoy watching Sidney Crosby. He's such an unbelievable talent and to come back from the concussions and hit his straps immediately is something to behold.

Ed Johnston
Somerset, England
New York Rangers

Wendel Clark - he came from a town of 200 people, and used effort and energy and became a folk-hero; he played above his size fighting much bigger players. Doug Gilmour - another small for the NHL player who used skill and effort to prove himself. Ed Jovanovski - came to hockey late, but boy could he skate!

Elliott Hall
Sheffield, England
Toronto Maple Leafs

The one and only Scott Stevens... because of his though play on the ice (his hits were... well... real ice hockey hits) and because of his blue eyes...

yes, I had a crush on him when I was a teen (and still have)...Marty Brodeur, because he's playing for the Devils since I became fan and because he is The Goalie! Petr Sykora, Jason Arnott and above all Patrik Elias: the Devils A-line of the second Stanley Cup win. Patrik still is one of my favourite players, I really don't know exactly why... maybe because of his style or because he's European or because I like his wife...Jonas Hiller: my second favourite goalie... I have to admit that I didn't follow him before Vancouver 2010, but after having seen his play during the Olympic Games I've been impressed by his style and I've thought he would have become the second best goalie in the NHL... after Marty of course! Pavel Datsyuk because he's the best two-ways forward of the league, it's a pleasure watching him play.

Emanuela Pozzi
Cernusco sul Naviglio, Italy
New Jersey Devils

Wayne Gretzky because he's the great one of course & from the sabres I'd say either Tyler Ennis or Tyler Myers (Marcus Foligno is coming close though after what we've seen of him) but in the league overall I'd say Malkin because he has everything you'd want in a forward

Gareth Dutton
Manchester, England
Buffalo Sabres

Well this list could go on and on! But to narrow it down to a few past and present I'm going to go with. Scott Stevens - one of the biggest hitters to ever lace the skates always a fan favourite and awesome to watch just waiting for him to deliver a bone crusher of a hit. And Scott Niedermayer one of the greatest skaters would just glide across the ice effortlessly and brought a great offensive aspect from the defence. Present, I'm going to go with David Clarkson, just love the way he plays so full of heart never scared to drop the gloves or stick up for a team mate wins most of his battles along the board and now I'm so pleased for him that his scoring has picked right up with his best season to date so far.

Gavin Clarke
Bristol, England
New Jersey Devils

I have 2 favourite players who are currently playing for the Stars in the NHL. The first one is centreman Jamie Benn. It is incredible to think that the 2011/12 campaign was just his third season of NHL hockey. This guy has huge amounts of talents and I believe he will be one of, if not the best players in the NHL in a few seasons as he builds up experience. He never fails to produce highlight reel goals, but for me, it is his work off of the puck that singles him out from other centres in the league. He is definitely one to watch in the next few seasons. My other favourite player is the Stars' starting goaltender, Kari Lehtonen. Words can't describe how awesome he was in the 2011/12 season. His stats aren't anything special, but are up there with the better goaltenders. What impresses me most is the way he maintains a very good save percentage despite being given a much bigger workload than the average starting goalie. The Stars have struggled to find a consistent back-up goalie, meaning the pressure has been piled onto Kari's shoulders on a regular basis. Last season he pulled off some saves that you had to watch 10 times over to see how he kept the puck out of the net. He has now definitely gained the 'elite' status and could see himself being the best in the league in a few years time.

George Royle
Malmesbury, England
Dallas Stars

Curtis Joseph - I've always been fascinated by netminders and whilst he may not have been one of the best to ever lace 'em up, he always had an atmosphere of "underdog" about him. My first Leafs jersey was a Cujo shirt and I sulked for a week when he signed for the Redwings. Gary Roberts - In the dictionary, under the definition for Hockey Player it says "See Gary Roberts". Complete warrior mentality and just about unstoppable - like "The Terminator" on skates. Tomas Kaberle - Complete opposite to Gary Roberts (someone once remarked that "he's never found a corner that he liked"), but plays with skill and patience. A huge inspiration on my game when I played Rec hockey (and one of the reasons I used to wear "15")

Gord Turner
Manchester, England
Toronto Maple Leafs

I loved Grant Fuhr. At the time I was getting into the Blues, we had Cujo and Jon Casey in net, but I wasn't taken with either. Fuhr was in a great tandem with Hasek in Buffalo and things were great. Later on, we acquired him in the 1995-96 season and I was sold! He made 76 consecutive starts in net and was part of that great Hull/Gretzky season. His movement round the crease and his athleticism utterly blew me away. Then came Nick Kypreos and his cheap shot to destroy his knee. The sight of him limping and trying in vain to carry on with a blown knee only reinforced my love for him. My other love was Brett Hull. His sniping was legendary and a big reason on how I got into the Blues in the first place! Just to watch him whip the puck into the net from 20 feet away before the keeper even had chance to move cemented him as my favourite Blues player ever. My favourite non-Blues player has to be Neal Broten of the Minnesota North Stars/New Jersey Devils/Dallas Stars. A hard charging, no-quarter-given kind of player, his play in the 1996 Stanley Cup run for NJ will forever remain etched in my memory as he did it all. Scored, checked back, set up. He was all-action and I loved that,

Grant Sales
High Wycombe, England
St Louis Blues

Alex Ovechkin. Everything that he gets criticised for by the Canadian media is everything I love about him. I love how much energy he has and how much he celebrates. He plays the game with a smile on his face and there's nothing better than seeing how much scoring means to a player. I also love that he's not just about scoring, he can do it all, I love his massive hits just as much as his game-winning goals. My other favourite are the hardworking players like Brooks Laich, Jason Chimera and Matt Hendricks. They're all equally capable of coming up with massive goals but they also put their bodies on the line and give 100% every shift and don't mind not being in the spotlight.

Hana Imiolczyk
Merthyr Tydfil, Wales
Washington Capitals

The first one is probably far too obvious as a Penguins fan - Sidney Crosby. The way he plays is just breath taking to watch. The way he came back from his second concussion and scored points at such a rate. So scary to think we may not have seen his best season yet, the way he was dominating the league before the Winter Classic in 2011 was unbelievable! Secondly is Kris Letang, I've been a big fan of Tanger ever since he made the step up to the NHL. He must be the strongest skater in the league; it's just unbelievable how well he skates. Also for an offensive D man he plays pretty solid defence and he'll be a big part of the team for years to come hopefully!

James Bird
Burnley, England
Pittsburgh Penguins

Personally PA Parenteau, Matt Moulson and Nabokov have all impressed me this term for the Islanders but for me my favourite player is John Tavares! But as a fan of hockey I really admire Patrick Kane and Ovechkin, 2 quality hockey players

James Cartwright
Cardiff, Wales
New York Islanders

As a Leafs fan, I have to say Mats Sundin - consistent, goalscoring, dedicated Leafs legend. Also, Tie Domi for his fighting skills and willingness to take on far larger opponents. Of the current crop, Luke Schenn has the potential to develop into a solid Leafs defenceman who's enhancing his physical game and isn't afraid to stick up for teammates.

Jamie Mash
Northallerton, England
Toronto Maple Leafs

This is a dangerous question and could result in the list being ridiculously long. From the Canadiens' roster, my favourite players are Carey Price, Max Pacioretty, P.K Subban and Eric Cole. With Carey Price, I've been a fan of his since he made his debut. He's calm and collected and I think the rest of the NHL saw what a great character he is in the All Star Game. Pacioretty, what can be said: guy broke his neck and came back to score 30+ goal season. He has incredible talent and despite his injury he plays a fearless game. Other NHL players that I like are Marty St. Louis of the Tampa Bay Lightning, just because he has got some serious wheels on him and despite his small stature he never let that hold him back. He is the catalyst of the Tampa team and is just pure class on and off the ice. There's also Vincent Lecavalier who I like to watch, but he has had injury troubles that have prevented us from seeing his true skills the past few seasons. Then there are the NHL Finns that I follow. Saku Koivu, Teemu Selanne and Mikko Koivu are probably the ones I most follow and class as my modern favourites. But my all-time favourite player is Jari Kurri. I grew up watching him play and he inspired me to start playing.

Janne Virtanen
Hameenlinna, Finland (now Basingstoke, England)
Montreal Canadiens

Ice Hockey Nights in Europe

Tough question this, but I can say that I liked some of the hard-working 4th line grinders as well as the star players. How many should I choose? As a Sharks fan, you have to like Patrick Marleau – simply 'Mr San Jose Shark' as a one-club loyal man. He's still got that incredible speed too. Big Joe Thornton is a class act on and off the ice. Is there any better set-up man in the NHL? He seems to be getting better and tougher each playoff year too - developing into a real leader. Jonathan Cheechoo: the Cheechoo train is our first and only Rocket Richard winner to date in 2005-06 (and I have one of his game-worn jerseys!) with 56 goals. Great to also see him come back to the organisation last year with Worcester Sharks for a time. Others include Torrey Mitchell for 'that' goal he scored off his knees at Anaheim in Dec. 2007. I was watching it Stanley's Bar at Sharks ice on my first visit to San Jose, so it is memorable for me. (I also got it selected in the 'Ask Torrey Mitchell' segment on the Sharks website!). Got to mention Evgeni 'Nabby' Nabokov as well of course, Devin Setoguchi, Frazer McLaren and Brad Staubitz (best beatdown March 2009 v Tootoo, Nashville. Or is it just because I got these guys' jerseys too?

Jason Dunn
Woking, England
San Jose Sharks

I have always admired Ryan Smyth - he works so hard in the dirty areas of the ice. I'm also a big Sid Crosby fan - he is such a complete player, works hard on any areas he feels he is falling short in, is not afraid of going into corners and has such amazing skill.

Joan Chisholm
Washington, England
Edmonton Oilers

My favourite players would have to be Nicklas Lidstrom, Pavel Datsyuk, Henrik Zetterberg, and Niklas Kronwall. I love each of these guys for different reasons. Nicklas Lidstrom, because of his general all around greatness, his feel for the game, and the way he reads what's going to happen, so he can always be one step ahead. Pavel Datsyuk for the way he can make getting past half a team's line on his own look easy, and the way he can score beautiful goals in high pressure situations. Zetterberg for the fact that he is an all around great player, and can improve any line he is on tenfold. Finally, I love Niklas Kronwall because, firstly, he is a solid defenceman, and secondly, because I just love the power of his open ice hits. My favourite goalies of all time would have to be Patrick Roy (despite his role for the Avs in the Wings/Avs rivalry) and Tim Thomas. Both of these guy are fantastic goaltenders that play with the passion that suggests that they want nothing less than a shut out, each and every game they play.

Joe Alderson
Stoke-on-Trent, England
Detroit Red Wings

Pavel Datsyuk - my favourite Red Wings player, he has the skills and pose as forward that sometimes has me thinking are you serious? Evgeni Malkin is something else everything he touches seems to turn into something special.

Junaid Hussain
Nottingham, England
Detroit Red Wings

If I was to pick one player, it would be Simon Gagne. I first noticed him at the Olympics in 2002 and now I'm definitely one of his biggest and most devoted fans (I even run a website - simongagne.com). His hockey skills are unique to me - his flawless skating, nifty passes, excellent vision on the ice, amazing snap shot, wrist shot and exceptional defensive play. The fact he can play on both power play and penalty kill and excel at both. Love his ability to show up when it truly matters (see his overtime winners and playoff performances). His dedication to the team, to the game, to the fans. Despite not being quick to drop the gloves he won't hesitate to stand up for his teammates or himself if it's needed. He simply has all the qualities I value in a hockey player the most. Indisputably, his off ice manners are as well a big reason why Simon is my favourite. Always generous, kind and nice to whomever gets to meet him. He never hesitates to give an interview, give an autograph to a fan or take a picture with them. He gives back to the community, donating to charities. To name other few players I like – Martin St. Louis, Vincent Lecavalier, Mike Richards, Steven Stamkos and others.

Katerina Brzonova
Zlin, Czech Republic
Tampa Bay Lightning

Sidney Crosby: possibly the reason I got into hockey in the first place. His style of play has a fantastically striking fashion, which is a joy to watch. The tricks and actions of him on the ice make the game come alive for most. Sidney off-ice is something that is a joy to read about too. His charity work, determination and focus make him a fabulous role model for many hockey

Ice Hockey Nights in Europe

fans across the world.

Katrina Gordon
Glasgow, Scotland
Pittsburgh Penguins

There are a number of players I like and admire from around the league and from within both of the teams I follow, but I'd like to dedicate this answer to one man: a man who quietly goes about his business without any fuss. An unsung hero; a man who flies under the radar of the sporting media as possibly the most under-appreciated all-around athlete in the league. He's that guy in every team who works away in the background and never get the recognition they deserve until they are no longer around. Am I exaggerating? Perhaps, but he's worth it. It's the altogether splendid Captain of the New York Rangers, Ryan Callahan. Why do I revere the god that is Captain Cally so much? Myriad reasons. He's first and foremost a great leader and a massive presence for the Rangers both on and off the ice. He may not be the loudest voice in the dressing room but he is certainly one of the most respected. His commitment is unequalled: he gives 100% in every game and to every element of the game – he skates with ease and speed, he hits hard yet cleanly, he can pick out a shot so sweet it makes goalies weep. He is the beating heart and passionate soul of the New York Rangers and you can foresee his jersey being raised to the roof years down the line. He's been in the middle of everything good that has happened for the Rangers this season and when he's missing you sure as hell know about it. He is game-changer, a clutch player, and a stand-up guy. Everything you want for your favourite sportsman, your team Captain, and your most admired athlete. Captain Cally, I salute you.

Katy Parles
Newcastle Upon Tyne, England
Calgary Flames

I'd like to answer this with a past and present, I mean it's easier for me that way. In the past, my favourite players have been Mario Lemieux and Joe Sakic, it's weird for me as a Kings fan since neither of the players even played for L.A. and stuck with their single team/franchise for their entire careers, but the respect I have for them is very high. With Lemieux, he's arguably one of the best players in the game next to Gretzky, but what strikes me the most about him is his dedication to the team, both during and even after his career. His battle with Hodgkin's disease would have taken anyone out of the game and into retirement but #66 came back and carried on his love for the game, and even after retirement he made sure to keep the Pens in Pittsburgh by even becoming owner and player of the team, which takes a lot of dedication and respect. Not to mention he's the sole player in the NHL to score all the different kinds of goals in a single game, something Gretzky never did and I like to think that if Lemieux didn't suffer injury or Hodgkin's then he may well have passed Gretzky in the all time points section. With Sakic, he's a class act in every sense of his personality, the quiet leader who leads on the ice without even having to say a word when on it, and being the Captain of the Nordiques and Avalanche for as long as he was commands respect, but to me the most defining action of his that earned my respect was the 2001 Cup Finals, having not deciding to skate with the Cup first, handing it immediately to Bourque and finally letting the veteran D-man finally achieve his dream after his long career, when I watched the video of it on YouTube it nearly brought a manly tear to my eyes because it was just a beautiful moment you could only ever see in ice hockey and no other sport.

Kenny Jones
Caernarfon, Wales
LA Kings

Patrice Bergeron. Very under rated player, a top 2-way forward who can read the game like no other. Pavel Datsyuk - Who does not love to watch what Datsyuk does? He is magical with the puck. Tim Thomas- Wow, Flashy saves, aggressive goal tending, and even logged a hit on Henrik Sedin.
Shawn Thornton - Not the most skilled guy by a long way, but has so much heart and effort. His hits, and fights can singlehandedly change a game. Also, did you see his penalty shot this year? He looked like Datsyuk out there.

Kimmi Noble
Sheffield, England
Boston Bruins

My favourite player is definitely Frans Nielsen of the New York Islanders. Of course he's a Dane, but it's not just about that. It's about his skill. He's ability to read the game. His backhand. His modesty. And well, maybe it's also about him being the first Dane making it to the NHL.
He seems like such a low key Juttlander (Juttland is the part of Denmark where he's from), with both feet, planted solidly on the ground. I love that he sticks up for his team, as I think many of the other Islanders player do. He and they believe in their team, and know it's a good team. He's dangerous shorthanded, in the shootout, on the powerplay kill, and he

knows how to get to the net with the puck.

Kristina Stryhn Laursen
Copenhagen, Denmark
Toronto Maple Leafs / New York Islanders

There is no the biggest Daniel Alfredsson's fan in Poland than me. Alfredsson is Captain of the Ottawa Senators, one of the greatest player in the league, and - for sure - the biggest star of the franchise history. Alfredsson is this type of player I like the most. Leading by example, fantastic leader, one of the most dynamic player in NHL. He has all the tools you want to from player in this league. He's not only fantastic player, but in my opinion he's great man.

Krzysztof Sankiewicz
Warsaw, Poland
Ottawa Senators

My favourite players would include Wayne Gretzky, Sidney Crosby, Mats Sundin and Gordie Howe, all for differing reasons. I could name lots of others but my favourite player would be goaltender Johnny Bower. This guy played with poor eyesight and in the day, goalies had barely any protective gear including no mask! Calling him brave would do this legend an injustice. He played from 1945-1970, only starting to play Junior hockey after returning early from action in World War 2. He won 3 AHL Championships as well as 4 Stanley Cups in his career and played until the ripe old age of 45. He was a Hall of Famer 9 times over! He won 706 games, Vezina Trophy winner twice and won his last Stanley Cup at 42 years of age. More than all the accolades and his fantastic career, Johnny Bower is a fantastic human being. Never doing enough for charity and young kids. He has always appreciated the support of Leaf fans from his playing days until the present day. So much so that he will always make himself available for events held for the fans and never refuses an autograph or a photo. That bond between him and us, the fans, makes him my favourite ever player.

Mark Rackham
Kent, England
Toronto Maple Leafs

For me my favourite player has to come from my favourite NHL team the Coyotes, simply put it's Shane Doan. This guy is Mr Coyotes, he has been part of the organisation since its last year in Winnipeg. Throughout his career he has stuck with the Coyotes through the many up's and down's and has now iced close to 1,200 NHL games. He has to be considered as a future hall of famer, not least through the number of games played, but also, for his loyalty. There is not much of that in pro sports, but there are a select few! My other pick for a player worthy of recognition is Martin St. Louis, one of the shortest guys on the ice but anything but in terms of his play and value to the Tampa Bay Lightning. He is a perfect example of a player who doesn't let his size hinder his game. His almost telepathic link with Vinny Lecavalier lead the Bolts to a Stanley Cup too!

Mark Woodcock
Macclesfield, England
Phoenix Coyotes

My favourite current player is Evgeni Malkin; he has a grace on the puck that no other player can equal. He makes everything look effortless and the way he can skip from carrying the goalscoring load to being the playmaker shows just how versatile he is! Mats Sundin is a Leafs legend and rightly so, he carried the whole team on his shoulders and it's no coincidence that the Maple Leafs are a shell of a team since he left - how can you not love a player like that? Other than that, I have a lot of respect for Trevor Linden who always comes across as a true ambassador of the game, and then of course there's Gretsky, whole books have been written about him, but suffice it to say that he transcends the game and holds records I don't see anyone beating in my lifetime...

Matt Merritt
Portsmouth, England
Toronto Maple Leafs

I have many favourite players who have come and gone over the years but I have put them all down to three. My all-time number one player is Mats Sundin, former captain of the Toronto Maple Leafs and an important player of the Swedish national team for almost 20 years. He did score a lot in his career and he was one of the NHL's best players a couple of years. He accomplished an average of more than one point per game. But this is not why I like him the most. My respect did he get by his way of acting on the ice. He always put the team first and the way he celebrated his and his teammates goals was uplifting. His smile has brought happiness to many Swedish living rooms over the years. I also have to mention the look in his eyes when Sweden completed a turnaround against Finland from 1-5 to a win by 6-5 in the 2003 World Championships. What a warrior! My second favourite player is Valeri Kamensky. I started to like him before he went to the NHL in the early 90's. He played in the Sovjet Union's national team in the late 1980's and I remember watching him on TV. I can't recall what it was in his way of playing that I liked but think it was that he scored a lot and mostly in a pretty way. Finally I have to include my favourite Avalanche player. No 25, Shjon Podein . He wasn't the most technical player but his night in and night out effort in the Avs jersey got my attention and the way he was killing penalties along with Stephane Yelle was amazing. I especially remember one game when I was working night shift, listening to an Avs game over the internet in which Podein scored a shorthanded goal by stealing the puck from Dallas Stars goalie Ed Belfour and sealed the deal in overtime.

Mattias Boström
Stockholm, Sweden
Colorado Avalanche

Miikka Kiprusoff - inspiring; Michael Cammalleri - no nonsense; Sidney Crosby - the full package; Tim Thomas - professionalism

Melanie Warn
Devon, England
Calgary Flames

My favourite player nowadays is, hands down, Claude Giroux. He has the talent but also the hockey IQ and mentality that make a NHL great. He wants to play the game, he's really into it. The thing I just love about him is his commitment to the team. He wants to be the game changer and if he's not, he really shows his frustration. He's not afraid to take one for the team, to throw out crunching hits, to go to the dirty areas, to backcheck... It's incredible to see how he matured since he was drafted. Funny, how he went from „the kid, whose name couldn't even be remembered" to the Flyers' saviour and go-to guy. G is just fun to watch, every time he's playing he catches your eye with something fancy. A beauty heads up pass here, a dangle through 2 defensemen there. My 3 favourite players that I grew up to idolise are Peter Forsberg, Joe Sakic and Patrick Roy. Pretty obvious, again. Why? First, they are Avalanche legends (even though Sakic was the only career-long Avalanche), second, they pretty much resemble everything a team needs to be successful: the natural leader and face of the franchise (Sakic), the talented & skilled one (Foppa), the cocky game-changing goalie (Roy). I loved Sakic for his leadership, his attitude on the ice, his hard work, his class, but it wasn't just that. Burnaby Joe was just as skilled as he was a great leader, racking up 1,641 points in 1,378 games, 625 of them being goals. The reason I loved Foppa was the fact, that he was a constant threat when on the ice. To the ones who disagree, go watch his 3+3 game against the Panters in which he single-handedly led a comeback from 5-0 to 5-7. Too bad his career was cut just to 708 games....Patty Roy is also obvious, for me the best tender to ever play the game (save for Ken Dryden and Bernie Parent).

Michal Hežely
Michalovce, Slovakia
Colorado Avalanche

I don't have an active favourite player. Markus Naslund is retired for a while now, but nobody really replaced him. I like the Sedin's a lot - the way they play when on their game is pure poetry - but you look for that special something in a player. Hard to say what it is. I have a soft spot for Swedish hockey style and I'm a Canuck at heart, so I guess I will have to wait until the Canucks draft some next Swedish superstar! I guess Danish could be close enough to Swedish, so here's hoping Nicklas Jensen will break out big. I seek for intelligence and leadership qualities in players. And they have to play big. This is why I'm developing a soft spot for Claude Giroux - a classic example of a star who makes others around him better. He's fun to watch, very intelligent with the puck, very emotional. Great leader too. He has all the qualities but one - he's not a Canuck. In all seriousness, one can't have everything.

Michał Pręgowski
Warsaw, Poland
Vancouver Canucks

Peter Forsberg is my hockey idol, I really admired the way he played the game. Not only was "Foppa" a superb playmaker but also he combined his insane offensive skills with the physicality and intensity of a grinder. It's a shame that his career was so hampered by injuries, the fact he only played around 700 games in the NHL is a travesty. I see a lot of those traits in Gabriel Landeskog and Ryan O'Reilly, my two favourite players on the current Avalanche roster, both have big futures ahead of them. From the rest of the league, Scott Niedermayer was a superb defenseman, but also a real leader and that showed in his playoff performances. He was a guy that fans from other teams had great respect for, me included.

Mike Fuller
Newcastle, England
Colorado Avalanche

Ice Hockey Nights in Europe

My favourite all time player is Peter Forsberg because I think the guy was just a warrior. To top it off he was the most talented player of his era and his love for the game was unprecedented. Mats Sundin and Teemu Selanne come in close second. Nikolai Kulemin and Mikhail Grabovski are my two favourite Leafs right now, with my two favourite Penguins being Gino (Evgeni Malkin) and MAF (Marc-Andre Fleury). If I had to choose one current player, it would have to be Gino because he seems like such a goofball (is smarter than he looks) and his team first attitude and the will to win gets underappreciated at times. Peter Forsberg will most probably remain my all time favourite athlete.

Mislav Jantoljak
Zagreb, Croatia
Pittsburgh Penguins / Toronto Maple Leafs

My favourite player is a goalie, his name is Peter Budaj. I discovered the NHL because of Peter. I love his game, his team, he is the first goalie that I discovered in the NHL because I like Slovakia and Slovak players. I was able to meet him last year and he is a super guy. I saw him play against Washington at the Bell Centre, I made the trip to Montreal from France to meet him. I'm a fan of his team spirit. He supports his players a lot. I think he does not play enough this year with Montreal but I'm so proud of him.

Natacha Laporte
Strasbourg, France
Colorado Avalanche

I have to start with Vincent Lecavalier, so much talent and skill, just watch the 'through the legs' goal he scored against the Habs in the 2004 Stanley Cup run. Proud that he is our captain. How can you not love Marty St Louis, told he was too small for the NHL, undrafted out of college, dumped by the Flames, to go on to win a Stanley Cup and Hart Trophy. He is the heart and soul of the Lightning, and he just keeps getting better. You also have to have a soft spot for the two young superstars we have: Steven Stamkos just keeps getting better, has the best shot in the business and is becoming a leader on the ice, already two 50 goal seasons and he is only 22. The other is Victor Hedman, the European in me enjoys cheering him on, he is getting better with age and will be a rock for us as he ages.

Nathan Cartmel
Bristol, England (now Tampa, FL, USA)
Tampa Bay Lightning

Jonathan Northall

My favourite players are pretty varied I guess. Lets start with the Blackhawks, my team and my passion. I first started following hockey in the early 90s so obviously the first players I started to admire were Ed Belfour, Chris Chelios and Jeremy Roenick. Those guys were the core of a wonderful era....narrowly missing out on a Stanley Cup....Belfour was The Eagle, a complete goaltender who captured Veniza's with his effortless performances between the pipes....Chelios & Roenick were incredible to watch....Chelios is still a top 50 all time player for me....even into his Red Wing days. Roenick was always outspoken and passionate as well as an outstanding goal scorer. Going back to the 1960s, two of my favourite players of all time have to be Bobby Hull & Stan Mikita. Both have been constant nominees in hockey's top 100. Both players had a beautiful skating style and were masters of stick handling in a local golden time for the Hawks....I am a keen autograph collector and not surprisingly these guys feature many times in my collection. At the moment, my favourite Hawks are Brent Seabrook, an Olympian, SC winner and all round top blue liner who plays tough and contributes hugely to the fast flowing offensive hockey style of Quenneville's team. Non-Hawk players like many are Gretzky, Lemieux and Messier....these players were natural leaders of men and possessed talent like nothing else seen in the sport

Nathan Hollis
Norwich, England
Chicago Blackhawks

Favourite players. Not sure if this means on my team or in general so I'll do both just in case. Flyers - Claude Giroux. He has great puck moving skills, and one of the best passers in the game. It's been a long while since we've had one of the leagues super stars in orange and black. Is a joy to watch. Wish he'd shoot more though. Kimmo Timonen is 'Mr Reliable' at the back. Had a great career and a true warrior. The guy plays injured all the time and rarely looks a liability for it. When Pronger went down, we at least knew we had another #1 guy to take on the load. Todd Fedoruk - blast from the past this one. I loved 'the Fridge', he wasn't scared of anyone and had some epic battles for us. He had his demons off the ice, but they didn't seem to show on the ice. Every goal he scored was a bonus. For other teams, how can anyone not like Teemu Selanne? The guy just oozes class and is a mighty fine goalscorer. Him finally winning his cup is my 2nd favourite, non-Flyers hockey memory. My favourite non-Flyers hockey memory was watching Ray Bourque lift his cup. Another classy guy that deserved his name on the trophy. From what I can gather he was close to being a Flyer to, before Boston decided that the Colorado offer was a better fit for them. I remember willing him through that last shift of the final that year, which must have been about two minutes long as the Avs wouldn't let him change. Cal Clutterbuck: this guy should be a Flyer. He would be accepted in Philly purely for his 'can hit, will hit' attitude.

Ray Skeates
Basingstoke, England
Philadelphia Flyers

From the current Bruins line up, it's Chara. Historically, doesn't every Bruins fan name Bobby Orr? I guess every Blaze fan would probably name Wade Belak too, taken from us far too soon.

Richard Hardy
Hinckley, England
Boston Bruins

Tradition dictates that you choose a favourite player who is either as current member of your team's roster or once wore the cherished jersey that you support. Supporting a team like the Pittsburgh Penguins it would be easy to pick any of the great players to have graced the black and gold from 'Le Magnifique' through to 'Sid the Kid'. It would also be easy to pick from the many unsung heroes of a team, the players whose support play, back checking, blue line play or penalty killing skills enabled the great ones to flourish. Out of this list one man for me rises to the fore, a player who rose to stardom playing alongside one of the greatest of all time. He filled the left wing role with such power and skill he amassed 123 points in a season that saw him be only one of 3 players to outscore the Great One in a regular season (and he was only second behind his team mate that year). Over the 2 years of back-to-back Stanley Cup wins for Pittsburgh (90-91 & 91-92) he played in every single regular season and playoff game. Four straight seasons of 40 goals, including one of 50 goals reinforced his shooting prowess. Hockey skills alone are not what make Kevin Stevens my favourite player. A year after lifting the Stanley Cup he suffered a terrible injury on the ice, clashing heads in a game then landing face first on the ice shattering his skull. Reconstructive surgery using metal plates to rebuild his skull was followed by long period of rehabilitation that would have tested any professional sportsman. His desire to play led him to return to the ice the following year where he once again posted a 40+ goal season just falling short of 100 points. Sadly this success was not to continue and battled drink and drug addictions. His career suffered and he moved around the teams trying to find a place where he could rediscover what he had in Pittsburgh but he was unsuccessful. Ice time became limited and the points disappeared. He returned to Pittsburgh for one last season where he showed some of the class he was known for but time was catching up with him. The Penguins then offered him a scouting role, which he took. His desire to play, ability to overcome everything thrown in his path and gritty determination on the ice to fight for the win are what makes Kevin Stevens my favourite player.

Rob Aherne
Stafford, England
Pittsburgh Penguins

A couple of very predictable responses, one that kind of makes sense and then one right out of left field. #66 Mario Lemieux is without a doubt my favourite player of all time. Strange when I tell you that I have only seen him play once and that when I first became a hockey fan he was at the time retired from the game. My love of Le Manifique began on the night I became a Pens fan - Mario's return at the end of 2000 against Toronto. Having initially marvelled at his brilliance - thanks to the power of the internet - I then retrospectively became hooked on his story. From his early days in Pittsburgh, to the Stanley Cup wins, his battle with cancer and crippling back injuries and then onto him saving the team from bankruptcy and now steering the team through the choppy political waters to it's new home at the CEC. He is an Olympic Gold medallist, three Hart trophies, six Art Ross trophies, four Lester B Pearson awards, two Conn Smythe trophies, Masterton Trophy winner, numerous All-star games and awards....the list goes on. And had he stayed healthy I truly believe he would have challenged Gretzky's scoring records. For Mario is THE best of all-time. #9 Gordie Howe - let me start by saying I'm no Red Wings fan, you could possibly even add them to my teams I love to hate. Obviously given that I share a surname with Gordie, I was naturally drawn to him as I got into hockey. I've read a number of books about Mr Hockey and have become enthralled in his story. His records speak for themselves and boy what a list of records and achievements! I've been compiling my family tree for a number of years now and I keep hoping that I'm going to find some distant relative from the past left the UK to settle in Saskatchewan. #9 Paul Beraldo - who? I hear you ask. Drafted 139th by the Boston Bruins in 1986, Beraldo split the 87-88 and 88-89 seasons between the Bruins and their AHL affiliate of the time the Maine Mariners. During this time the native of Hamilton, Ontario played 10 games in the NHL but failed to register a single point. After the 89-90 season Beraldo moved to Europe and spent a number of years playing in Italy before making the DEL in 1995. He won the DEL a year later with Adler Mannheim, but then having spent a year in

Switzerland the Canadian and Italian national team player found himself on the fabled Sheffield Steelers Grand Slam winning team from the 00-01 season. As a Sheffield Steelers fan I loved watching Paul play, scoring many goals from the right wing circle with a blistering one-time shot. Sadly, he sustained an injury during a game against rivals Manchester Storm and missed a huge portion of the season. His return to the line-up sparked a notorious New Years Eve brawl as he sought retribution against Manchester's Corey Spring - the player who had injured him earlier in the season. More so for his style of play than his actual numbers, Beraldo is my favourite Steelers player of all-time.

Rob Howe
Sheffield, England
Pittsburgh Penguins

Without a doubt my favourite NHL player is Evgeni Malkin of the Pittsburgh Penguins. It is not only the obvious dominant play and physical presence of Geno that I admire, but also his background in a blue collar Russian town and his efforts to fit into American society. We all know that Malkin was the first Russian to win the Conn Smythe Trophy as playoff MVP in 2009, but more importantly for Pens fans was his leadership during Sidney Crosby's absence from January 2011 until March 2012. The 'Guins did not miss a beat during their captain's concussion injuries with Geno taking the helm. In fact, some Penguins fans (myself included), wonder why Evgeni isn't named team captain. The team seems to play better with #71 leading them. Being the son of a steelworker from Magnitogorsk, Russia has certainly won over the numerous Pens fans that have Steelers in their family. When Malkin took the Stanley Cup to his father's steel mill in the Summer of 2009 that was simply the greatest thing someone playing for a Pittsburgh sports team could do! Geno's slow yet steady progress with the English language is also an inspiration for me. I am also struggling horribly with learning Swedish ever since moving here, but when I see everyone smile when Malkin does interviews in English it gives me encouragement knowing that my Swedish is simple and childlike, yet people understand me just like they do with Evgeni.

Robert Campbell
Pittsburgh, USA (now Uppsala, Sweden)
Pittsburgh Penguins

My favourite player of the Ottawa Senators is their captain, Daniel Alfredsson. Alfie is a true leader, a veteran and an all-round classy guy, recently the crowd at Scotiabank Place can be heard chanting 'Alfie! Alfie!

Jonathan Northall

Alfie!' at the 11 minute mark in each period of each home game. My other players within the Ottawa team are Erik Karlsson, Jason Spezza (who lead the Sens in scoring) and building blocks of the team such as Chris Phillips and Chris Neil. They are committed to the franchise and put their heart and soul in to the game. As far as players from other teams go, I really enjoy watching Scott Hartnell and Jaromir Jagr from the Philadelphia Flyers and Pavel Datsyuk of the Detroit Red Wings

Robert Weaver
Gloucestershire, England
Ottawa Senators

I'll admit it – I'm a goalie fan. Their brains seem to be wired in an odd way to want to stand there whilst hard rubber is fired at them at 100mph. I have an "old time" favourite and a "current" favourite. Old time – it has to be Grant Fuhr. The guy just never gave up – even with a dodgy knee after that collision with Nick Kypreos he still became one of the three winningest goalies in Blues history. For current players, it's Jaroslav Halak. Jaro seemed to come from nowhere to help the Canadiens to that fantastic playoff run in the 2009/2010 season. Expectations were high when he joined the Blues – too high in some cases. One thing seems certain – Jaro needs a strong backup to push him. The Blues now have that – and Jaro has shown this year why the Blues traded for him. I love the guy – every time he's counted out, he comes back stronger.

Sandra Pascoe
Penzance, England
St Louis Blues

I love a lot of players. Basically two whole roster of Winnipeg Jets and Philadelphia Flyers. My favourite forward is Claude Giroux, no question about that. He's amazingly talented. I have all the respect for the guys like Malkin, Crosby, Lundqvist and I am able and glad to admit they are the best ones of this league but... I can't bring myself to liking them because they are on the teams I dislike, I love Datsyuk though, there is nothing about him to dislike. He's a magician.

Štěpánka Černá
Dolní Němčí, Czech Republic
Winnipeg Jets

Rick Nash is unsurprisingly my favourite player of all-time. A number one draft pick in 2002, he is supremely talented and was the face of the Blue Jackets for a long time. He added legitimacy to what was a perpetually struggling organisation and if he left with most fans' blessing. He deserves to be at a team capable of winning the Stanley Cup, and the Blue Jackets are anything but that at the moment. RJ Umberger is another of my favourites. He has been a good acquisition for the Blue Jackets and also has history with the city of Columbus, having played college hockey for Ohio State University. My initial interest in hockey was sparked when I lived in Switzerland and as such, I keep track of Swiss players such as Mark Streit of the New York Islanders, Jonas Hiller of the Anaheim Ducks and Yannick Weber of the Montreal Canadiens. Luca Sbisa is my favourite of the Swiss contingent as he was drafted in the first NHL draft I followed and is from the same Swiss village that I lived in.

Steve McCaskill
Maidstone, England
Columbus Blue Jackets

My favourite player on the Kings is Dustin Brown. He typifies for me what an all-round hockey player should be – scores goals, defensively sound and throws the body about (usually in league top 5 for hits over a season). Love watching him play. Outside of the Kings, it's Tim Thomas of Boston. He's got a madcap, unorthodox style but it works, and ultimately, that is what is required from a netminder.

Stuart Coles
Coventry, England
LA Kings

In regards to my team, favourite players come in the shape of Bob Probert, Steve Yzerman and Nick Lidstrom. Probert played the game with pure heart and soul, Yzerman with incredible skill and ability, whilst Lidstrom is a picture of measured precision and calm. In terms of the game as a whole, it's tough not to mention Wayne Gretzky as possibly the best player to lace up skates. High on my admiration list are goalies Henrik Lundqvist and Tim Thomas, defencemen Zdeno Chara and Duncan Keith, and forwards Jeff Skinner, Evgeni Malkin and Wayne Simmonds. All are guys who hold their respective teams together, be that with a moment of sublime skill, or with a heart-on-sleeve attitude to do the very best until the final horn.

Stuart Wilson
York, England
Detroit Red Wings

Jonathan Northall

I don't actually have a favourite player. Pretty much anyone who wears the orange and black really. Though I have to say that my favourite all-time player is Ron Hextall. One of many names I remember from my younger days. His stands out more for some reason. Perhaps it was his influence that made me want to play in goal for my primary school field hockey team!

Tim Barnes
Cambridge, England (born in New Jersey, USA)
Philadelphia Flyers

My all time favourite player, is probably most NHL fans least favourite player, Sidney Crosby. He's captain of the Penguins for starters and is, in my opinion, the best player in the game. He's lived up to his name 'the next one', won everything there is to win and he's still young. He gets a lot of stick, mainly from Flyers fans, for being soft and a cry baby, but he's matured so much since his first few years in the NHL, when he was that type of player. Despite missing 10 months with a concussion he's managed to come back and pick-up where he left off and if he stays concussion free, should lead the Penguins to many more victories.

Tom Harding
Isle of Wight, England
Pittsburgh Penguins

As a Maple Leafs fan my favourite player would be Doug Gilmour. He epitomized the view that the regular measurable stats that scouts looked for in prospects were meaningless when compared with the will to win. He was always told he was too small to play much less succeed in the NHL and as such was taken in the lower rounds of the draft. I've never seen determination like it in a player since, hence his nickname "Killer." I've also become very interested in Ken Dryden after reading his book, The Game. He seems to me to be the last truly great goaltender that didn't have the oversized body armour equipment that those after him had access too. He appeared to be the lynchpin of that 1970's Canadiens team. When he was on a sabbatical in 1974 and 1975, they lost out to the Flyers and when he retired in 1979 the Islanders broke through to become the dominant force in the NHL, the Habs wouldn't win again till Patrick Roy came along.

Tom Mannington
London, England
Toronto Maple Leafs

Ice Hockey Nights in Europe

My favourite current Leafs player is Joffrey Lupul. He has obvious the skills and has put up great numbers this season for a struggling team. However for me it is more a case of sensing how much he enjoys his hockey and how committed he seems to the Leafs. He also has a great relationship with the fans. All time player - I've usually had lots of affection for goalies so I would have to go for Martin Brodeur who I thought had a very cool name and mask when I first noticed him as a teenager but has also consistently been one of the top goalies in the NHL for many years now. I also once bought a signed Brodeur photo, which was mounted on a plaque many years ago from the American eBay web site. Cost a fortune in shipping I seem to remember!

Tony Harrison
Rutland, England
Toronto Maple Leafs

My favourite players on the Wild are Niklas Backstrom, Mikko Koivu, Josh Harding, Cal Clutterbuck & Matt Cullen. Backstrom is just great, the amount of games this guy has kept us in is unbelievable. Not to bad for an undrafted player. I'm absolutely sure that if he were to play elsewhere in a different system, he'd still put up good numbers, but heaven forbid that happens. Mikko Koivu - our first full time captain and he lead by example. Unfortunately he has been plagued by injuries in the past few years, but when he is in the lineup, he is one of the most underrated players in the league. Josh Harding - the perfect backup. He'd be a starter for a few teams in this league already, and may get his chance to prove it in the summer. Has had good numbers and team seem to have confidence in him when Backstrom gets his rest. Cal Clutterbuck - the guy just hits anything and everything. I love his physicality and how he can grind down opponents on every shift. He's pretty handy on the scoring side to. Matt Cullen - good to see him in a Wild jersey. He's won his cup and has come home. He was also one of the stand out guys when I saw the Wild beat Tampere.

Vicki Morgan
Basingstoke, England
Minnesota Wild

Jonathan Northall

5 *WHAT IS YOUR BIGGEST SACRIFICE OR MOST COMMITTED ACT AS A DEVOTED FAN?*

Readers from North America are going to look at this chapter and think that all European fans do is complain about the time difference. If only the sleep deficiency angle was the only consideration when watching your team play. For me, the choice of room is paramount to watching the game successfully. Not waking my family, or the neighbours, is the first issue to deal with. The ramifications of getting this wrong at, say 2am, can be disastrous. Secondly, a too comfortable viewing position could invite the notion of sleep. Whether it is a comfortable chair or, heavens forbid, watching in bed could result in missing periods of play and waking at 4am with neck problems. I'm guessing that younger fans will find this less of a possibility but time will catch up with them too.

Your choice of team can also severely impact on your sleep patterns during the hockey season. Fans of Western Conference teams will take perverse pleasure in telling you that games start at 3am UK time (one or two hours later in Continental Europe). The problem doesn't resolve itself as a fan of Eastern Conference teams either. I think the key to survival during the season is to have a decent sleep strategy: no job or children would help too. Basically, it's best to resign yourself to the fact that four hours sleep, if you are lucky, is the best you'll get. Having negotiated the months of October to April on this basis, the playoffs bring a whole new challenge. Should a game go to double overtime, any notion of sleep is as good as gone. If this isn't bad enough, imagine staying awake through all of that just to lose the game....

Putting the sleep issue aside, there are so great stories contained in the chapter to demonstrate how much European fans love their team. For example, Raymond Jackson has gone to the lengths of putting his colours permanently on his body so there really is no hiding when the Flames lose badly.

Managing to convince my wife that it was a great idea to spend 10 days in Finland with my family at the start in October 2011, only letting slip at a later time that it just happened to coincide with the NHL Premier games in Helsinki! I don't think I'll ever live down this down from my wife, and I think it will be used in female mind games and manipulation to get her way until my dying day. Was so worth it though, not for the horrendously boring and disappointing game against Buffalo, but to see the Ducks play Jokerit, my childhood team. Something I will never forget, and something my wife will never let me forget either!

Allan Allison
Bristol, England
Anaheim Ducks

Watched every Boston Bruins playoff game of the 2010-2011 season into the early hours of the morning. So survived on only a few hours sleep for the duration of the Stanley Cup playoff but didn't miss a second. Well worth it.

Amy Hill
Camberley, England
Boston Bruins

I think the biggest sacrifice for hockey was staying up till 5 in the morning to watch a game between the Bruins and the Toronto Maple Leafs because my Internet went down so I stayed up for 2 hours till it came back on and then started watching it. Then at 7 in the morning I got up for university and sat an exam and went home to wait for my jersey to come in the mail. I then stayed up to watch another game that night. It doesn't seem like such a sacrifice but it took a lot out of me and had a rugby game the next day, it felt like a sacrifice on the field.

Callum Sweeting
Hull, England
Boston Bruins

As I'm a student, I'm yet to attend an NHL game as they're played during my university term time. However, the amount of cash I spend on merchandise, as well as staying up to the early hours (particularly if the Bruins are playing a west coast team) is the biggest sacrifice I have made. Although, staying up until 6am to watch the Bruins lift the Stanley Cup is definitely not a sacrifice in my eyes!

Kimmi Noble
Sheffield, England
Boston Bruins

Jonathan Northall

I watch games late at night, frequently records matches and watch the next day (trying not to know the score). Sometimes, my wife really hates me!

Bartek Pexu
Warsaw, Poland
Boston Bruins

Probably the same as for most European fans, staying up until 4 a.m. to watch my team play. Luckily I'm a collegian right now so I don't have to get up that early in the morning. I also spent a lot of money to see the Sabres play in Germany last fall, but I don't really see this as a sacrifice because it was an awesome experience and totally worth the money.

David Trippler
Mainz, Germany
Buffalo Sabres

Biggest sacrifice and most committed act as a fan of an NHL team in the UK, is lack of sleep you get, because you're staying up until 3-4am.

Gareth Dutton
Manchester, England
Buffalo Sabres

To answer your question my biggest sacrifice would have to be saving up and going over to Toronto to see the Flames play the Leafs at the ACC on the 14th March 2009 (which the Flames lost 8-6, gutted) or having 2 tattoo's, one on each arm of my beloved Flames

Raymond Jackson
Ballymena, Northern Ireland
Calgary Flames

Most committed is probably making the trip to Calgary whenever I can. Sacrifice - very little in comparison to the schedule of an NHL professional but my body clock takes a beating when staying up to watch the Flames play. Most of the matches don't start until 3am UK Time!

Melanie Warn
Devon, England
Calgary Flames

Time difference between Chicago and Finland is 8 hours, so in that case for example 6pm in Chicago is 2am in Finland. I go to school and I need some sleep and energy because of that, so I need to choose the games I watch pretty carefully. I watch games mostly on weekends and during the 5 day school week only if the game is special. During the playoffs, I watch each Hawks game and some other games too. When you add the World Championship games (which are a big thing in Finland) to that you get a sleep deprived and possibly very frustrated Blackhawks fan. Giving up sleep is probably the most devoted thing we Europeans do.

Satu Vanhanen
Joensuu, Finland
Chicago Blackhawks

Probably the project Eurolanche, but I could not say it is something like sacrifice. Everything what I am doing regarding to Colorado Avalanche is filling me with joy. I am responsible for the Eurolanche fan club what means I have to take care about our website 24/7 with other editors (3+ articles per day), organize meetings and do other activities. There are, of course, examples when I did not go to school after late night game.

David Púchovský
Bratislava, Slovakia
Colorado Avalanche

I think staying up throughout the night when I had work in the morning to watch various games that finished in the small hours.

Andy Parsons
London, England
Colorado Avalanche

The biggest sacrifice of every Europe-based NHL fan is sleep.
I'm no exception. I'm already used to it, not like I had any other option. As I stayed up more and more, I actually got used to it. Sometimes it doesn't work out. I overslept recently and was late for school because I stayed up to watch the play-offs. Not the first time I chose hockey over school! I find myself learning, doing homework at nights as I watch hockey. That results once again in hockey taking the upper hand and school being pushed aside. The other commitment is going home earlier than anybody else on a Friday evening, because of the games being played sooner.

Also, sometimes I don't sleep at all, mostly weekends because of the schedules (the first games begin at approx. 7 p.m. and the last end at 5 a.m.). So much for sleeping out at weekends!

Michal Hežely
Michalovce, Slovakia
Colorado Avalanche

The most committed act must be that night in 2001 when the Avs won their last Stanley Cup. I was in Oslo, working over the weekend at a sports event, and got my hands on a computer with Internet access. I spent the night in front of the screen whilst listening to the radio broadcast. I don't quite remember the time when I went to bed but I think that I got about two hours of sleep before it was time to get up to work again. I celebrated the whole day by wearing my white jersey. I also try to see as many games as I can but it is hard combining that with early working hours. The best thing I know is to get up about 4am and make myself a good cup of coffee, watch a great game of hockey, and then waking up the family before getting to school and work.

Mattias Boström
Stockholm, Sweden
Colorado Avalanche

The biggest sacrifice I have made for my team is sleep. As a relatively unfashionable team, the Blue Jackets make very rare appearances on British television, so I make a point of staying up for those, although I will watch a couple of the weekend games online live as well. As a student, it was perhaps less of a sacrifice, as I didn't sleep much anyway!

Steve McCaskill
Maidstone, England
Columbus Blue Jackets

For any fan based in Europe, the commitment of staying up late to watch a game (even if it isn't your team) is something I don't believe many other sports leagues have. Personally, my most stoic show of support was the 1999 Stanley Cup run for the Dallas Stars. Every game was televised on Channel 5. Games started between 10pm-12am and ran right through until 6-7am the next day. That, coupled with a heavy load I was facing at work, left me going 3 days without sleep at one point. I recall every single moment of the playoff run and can say loud and proud that to follow the Cup win, I amassed the grand total of 12 hours sleep across the whole 6-

game final series between the Stars and Sabres. I'm sure you can imagine how thrilled my boss was to hear that.

Chris Bluff
Stockton-On-Tees, England
Dallas Stars

I make sure I watch as many games live as I possibly can. The 3am games can be difficult and will admit to missing a few of those, but win or lose I stick through to the very end. Living this side of the Atlantic, it is very difficult to watch all 82 regular season games live, but I average 60-75 a season nowadays. Saturday nights are the real killer for me, as my own son has hockey training on a Sunday morning, which means waking at 5:30am and late nights are out. Hopefully, he repays my dedication by making it to the NHL himself.

Bradley Marsh
Essex, England
Detroit Red Wings

My biggest sacrifice would probably be the amount of money I have spent on jerseys, Gamecenter subscriptions as well as TV subscriptions, to keep watching the sport I love, although I don't consider this as much of a sacrifice, because it's something I love! My most committed thing as a fan would be sitting up, many nights, during each season, to watch the Red Wings play, despite often having to be awake early the next morning, to go to work, or any other things I may need to do. Though this is another thing I'm happy to do, for my love of the game.

Joe Alderson
Stoke-on-Trent, England
Detroit Red Wings

Reaching the playoffs has traditionally required the growing of an unruly and scruffy beard. Not only are my sleeping patterns regularly disrupted by late night live streaming, but adding a tramp-esque beard that makes me look like I have been living in a cardboard box for a week. I'm not counting saving up for years at a time to get a flight to the USA to watch live games.

Stuart Wilson
York, England
Detroit Red Wings

Jonathan Northall

That has to be the travel involved in getting to arenas - not just the away trips in Britain but also the trains in Poland, Greyhound buses in Boston, 5 people squashing into one taxi to get back to Vancouver - we are good at getting to places and not so good at planning our return.

Joan Chisholm
Washington, England
Edmonton Oilers

I've been a Florida Panthers fan since 2001 and this is my story of my dedication to them. Back in 2009 when the Florida Panthers released their 3rd jersey I tried to buy it from the NHL online store, but they wouldn't ship it to Scotland. As you could guess I wasn't very happy. The following February, my mum and I planned a trip to New York City. As soon as we got to our hotel the cases were dumped and off we went up 5th Ave to the NHL store. I got my jersey at last and my mum told me that the only reason we were in NYC was so I could get it. 6hrs on a plane, £2000 for flights and £600 for a hotel just to buy a jersey at $125. Quite possibly one of the most expensive jerseys owned by anyone. I think that's true dedication to my team.

Aimee Docherty
Port Glasgow, Scotland
Florida Panthers

Not going to lie, being a Western Conference fan has a downside, and being a Kings fan it's the worst downside. With a time zone that has a 8 hour difference, I sacrifice my sleeping patterns so much for the love of the game that I'll stay up most nights when the Kings are at home. I did it a lot during college, and watch the majority of the playoffs every year so my sleeping will have gone to hell anyway. On the college note, I can tell you that even though I stayed up until ungodly hours of 5-6am for the love of the game, I still woke up to go to college the same morning and ended up finishing with a really good grade (A- overall). Ultimately, I'd say my biggest sacrifices are sleeping hours when I was in college and still sacrificing the sleep even now, it's the love of the game and I wouldn't have it any other way until I have enough money to actually go to Los Angeles to catch a game wearing my customised jersey.

Kenny Jones
Caernarfon, Wales
LA Kings

Ice Hockey Nights in Europe

My biggest sacrifice is to my sleeping pattern! As a fan of one of the most western of the Western Conference teams, games face off generally around 3am local time. So I'm left with a choice; I could pull an all-nighter, but with 9am starts at work and 82 games in the regular season, playoffs on top – I wouldn't cope! Generally, I get up early before work so that I can watch the games on delay and then head on in…with a coffee in hand of course.

Stuart Coles
Coventry, England
LA Kings

I'd say that my biggest sacrifice following the NHL, let alone my team is the planet. I imagine most of the fans contributing to this book will have a similar story. 5 out of my last 6 holidays required me getting on a plane to see an NHL or AHL team. So my carbon footprint probably isn't that environmentally friendly. This saddens me because I like polar bears and penguins, but clearly I like hockey more. Trips to New York, Tampere, Belfast, Edinburgh & Stockholm to see 6 NHL teams including my beloved Wild and 2 AHL teams. The 6 holidays included spending some time in the Bridgestone Arena in Nashville, although not for hockey. Also made the pilgrimage to Toronto to see the Hockey hall of fame. Unfortunately we went in mid-April, so there wasn't any NHL hockey to watch. The Marlies were in San Antonio for a playoff series of their own, so had to settle for a baseball game. As fun as it was, it wasn't a patch on hockey. One top of this my purse took a hit to, not only for tickets for myself, hockey tickets are a great present for my fiancée. Anyone who knows me knows that this is a sacrifice!!! Getting to see any NHL game whilst living in Hampshire must count as a committed act.

Vicki Morgan
Basingstoke, England
Minnesota Wild

I suppose the biggest sacrifice I have made is staying up until 5 in the morning sometimes watching the Oilers or the Habs, if that's not a sacrifice this season with the way both teams played I don't know what is.

Diarmuid Murray
Dublin, Rep of Ireland
Montreal Canadiens

Jonathan Northall

My biggest sacrifice came probably in 2005-2006 season. At the time, I had a very poor Internet connection, so I didn't watch the games; I just listened to them on the radio. During the whole season, I listened to about 250 games of the NHL, AHL, QMJHL and the Memorial Cup combined. I was a huge, huge fan of Predators' superstar prospect Alexander Radulov, who was playing his second season with the Quebec Remparts (he finished regular season with 152 points in 62 games, and was fantastic in the playoffs and in the Memorial Cup tournament). I listened to Remparts' games on the Internet radio, in the middle of the night, even though they were in French, and I didn't know that language at the time. Sometimes I've gone two nights in a row without a second of sleep. Oh, those were the good times!

Paweł Jachowski
Siedlce, Poland
Nashville Predators

Well, sadly, living in England means I can't make it to games in person! But I do watch every game I can live online on TV and now on Gamecenter Live. Also, this means a lot of very late nights with the time difference and a very sleepy me in work the next day! So I feel that my main sacrifice as a fan in the UK is the sleep deprivation and making myself have a terrible day in work drinking copious amounts of coffee after a late night watching the Devils play.

Gavin Clarke
Bristol, England
New Jersey Devils

Sacrifice? Following my team is not a sacrifice even if sometimes can be difficult to. For now, I've not been able to travel to the US to watch live games. I've always been there on job travels with colleagues, and never had the possibility to take a night off to go to the arena. I've invested some money in jerseys and memorabilia, as all the real fans do! Luckily(?), I suffer from chronic insomnia so waking up and losing some hours of sleep in the middle of the night is not a real problem. One of my American friends told me some time ago while I commented on a blog that my alarm was already set as usual for the game time at 1am: "that's commitment!"

Emanuela Pozzi
Cernusco sul Naviglio, Italy
New Jersey Devils

Ice Hockey Nights in Europe

The biggest sacrifice I have had to make so far is staying up until ungodly hours watching my Islanders (especially when they take it to overtime, then shootouts and still lose!!) These late nights means I have missed few school lessons due to going to bed so late! Hopefully, I can save enough money up one day to visit Long Island and watch my beloved Islanders!!

James Cartwright
Cardiff, Wales
New York Islanders

I would say one of my biggest sacrifices is spending around about £250 on Rangers gear when I was in the NHL Store in New York! Another big sacrifice I made for hockey was watching Game 5 of the 2008 Stanley Cup Finals between the Detroit Red Wings and Pittsburgh Penguins. It was on Channel 5 and started just after midnight and there was a chance that the Cup was going to be won by the Wings, so I felt I had to watch it. It turned out to be a great game, ending 3-3 after regulation after the Pens scored with about 30 seconds left. What I had not bargained for is the game going to triple overtime, where the Pens finally won with a powerplay goal from Petr Sykora. At this point it was 5am. I didn't sleep after, got up at 6am and went to school and revised.

Daruish Gorgirzadeh
Bournemouth, England
New York Rangers

Actually, this is not really out of the ordinary but it's trying to find the games live. For a living, I lecture Law at university as well as writing a PhD, time is relatively scarce. If the Rangers play midweek I'll get up around 5.30am, fire Gamecenter up and watch the game before heading to work. However, for the playoffs I'll watch live. I'll make sure the diary is clear in the morning to allow a later start. I couldn't bear not knowing how they got on if I wasn't watching it live. I suppose, that's much most committed act although that will no doubt be overshadowed by other contributions!

Ed Johnston
Somerset, England
New York Rangers

Probably the same as most people's. Staying up late to follow countless NHL games. Even with work early the next morning, there's always a tough call to be made. I'm planning on visiting LA, New York and possibly

Jonathan Northall

Calgary soon, so hopefully I'll catch a game then if I get their during season time. The cost of that trip could really start to tally up if I include NHL games, but I'm sure it'll be worth it. I'm not sure if you'd call it a committed act, but I've also started a regular blog on the entire NHL with the help of a few other contributors.

James Willis
Watford, England
New York Rangers

My biggest sacrifice to the Ottawa Senators is my sleeping pattern, since becoming a hockey fan I no longer have one! I normally work evenings which allows me to catch up on sleep most of the time but on occasional can remember watching the Sens play against Vancouver at 3:00am and then had work at 7:00am. I can't say I was working at my best that day!

Robert Weaver
Gloucestershire, England
Ottawa Senators

To be honest with you, I have no idea. I'm Europe based fan so for people from Canada watching Senators' game at night is sacrifice. No big deal, they don't have this problem, they have our team all the time, at your fingertips.

Krzysztof Sankiewicz
Warsaw, Poland
Ottawa Senators

My biggest sacrifice as a devoted fan is probably my health. It wasn't meant out like that, originally it was just sleep, but led to other things. I try to stay up for every Flyers game, although for west coast games I'll nap before hand. My job means I'm up for 6:30-7:00am, so with games finishing around 2:30-3:00am it generally leads to less than 4 hours of sleep at night. I probably manage to watch all of about 80% of games. As a devoted fan, although as an NHL fan more than being a Flyers fan, I compile a spreadsheet each year full of statistics on each season. I've always been a stats guy even as a kid when I was introduced to football, and it carried over when I discovered hockey. Unfortunately I can't really do anything with it as I will no doubt infringe on copyright, but it can help when friends ask any questions. This year was the first year I tried to track the cap, not a true success as I struggled with calculating LTIR, but I often sent emails to Matt at Cap Geek advising him of call ups and demotions that they had initially missed. It felt great to help out a site, that has helped me and hockey fans

Ice Hockey Nights in Europe

all over the world since it's creation.
Providing my circumstances don't radically change, I expect that I will keep on doing this.

Ray Skeates
Basingstoke, England
Philadelphia Flyers

I would say the biggest sacrifice(s) I have ever made for my team would be the late nights staying up supporting the guys only to be walking round the office like a zombie the next day.
Also, when I lived in Toronto in 2009, I made the 1,000 mile round trip to Philadelphia for the 5 game home stance and in November 2007 I planned a two-week holiday to Toronto to coincide with a Flyers game, a 5 hour train ride away in Ottawa, which happened to be my first ever Flyers game (and we won!!).

David Lidbury
Bristol, England
Philadelphia Flyers

I'm fortunate that my team is based on the East Coast so that the time difference is only five hours. Nonetheless, I've stayed up for many games. Perhaps not as many as I should as a devoted fan, but I've done my share. I've travelled to the US to see my team play. Having booked my trip months in advance, the whole trip was almost scuppered due to the British Airways cabin crew strike. Fortunately, my flight went ahead (although it wasn't confirmed until 72 hours before it was supposed to go!). The trip turned out to be the best holiday I've ever had. Not just to the hockey and baseball, but the fact that everything just went well!
Though I suppose my most committed act is my duty as a moderator on the Official Flyers Message Board. The other members recommended my name, and I've been doing this since 2008.

Tim Barnes
Cambridge, England (born in New Jersey, USA)
Philadelphia Flyers

Not only do I stay up for at least 3/4th of the games my oh so poor team play which ruins my sleeping schedule (but also works to brainwash my kids as they see the end of the games in the morning) but I'm also saving enough money to go to Arizona, if the team doesn't relocate, and see a game or two.

Jonathan Northall

It's a pipedream but it's a good one.

Emil Rutkowski
Uppsala, Sweden
Phoenix Coyotes

Staying up to watch games. Staying up can be really tough at times, especially if you have a 9am commitment the next day. Often staying up hasn't gone to plan and I've woken up in the morning still in my office chair or sat up on the sofa because I've fallen asleep during the second intermission!
The tiredness the next day is always worse when the falling asleep didn't happen in bed!

James Bird
Burnley, England
Pittsburgh Penguins

Living in England makes it hard to watch the Penguins often, but when I heard they were playing in Stockholm, Sweden I knew I had to be there. I was keeping an eye on when the ticket details were announced and then all of a sudden they were sold out, before I even knew they were on sale. I managed to track some down on a website that had 2 tickets for the Penguins vs Ottawa game at £350 each, but that wasn't going to stop me!
I purchased the tickets, booked flights and literally flew out for the game and back the following morning - 24 hours later and £1,000 lighter - it was worth every penny!
My other most committed act as a fan was when I grew my playoff beard in 2009 and having to explain to every person why I had 2 months hair growth on my normally shaven face. Plus, the family were not pleased at my appearance at my niece's Christening 3 days before game 7 of the Stanley Cup final - I wasn't shaving for anything and it worked!

Tom Harding
Isle of Wight, England
Pittsburgh Penguins

My biggest sacrifice is sleep.
I imagine this is the major sacrifice most European fans will cite, purely because of the inherent time differences. I watch all 82 Penguins games live, whether they are in the East or West.
I've watched Penguins games on most continents, including secluded Thai beaches, with hill tribes in Cambodia, pool bars in the Caribbean, even on

Ice Hockey Nights in Europe

my Honeymoon!

Stephen Butler
Leicester, England
Pittsburgh Penguins

Sweden is six hours ahead of Pittsburgh so while Viasat Hockey shows the majority of Pens games here, most weeknight games start at 1:35am and end about 4am! I usually need to be up at 6:30am to attend my daily 8am "Swedish For Immigrants" classes, so unless it's a big rivalry game I would watch the replay the following afternoon and instead listen to Mike Lange and Phil Bourque call the action via the Penguins iPhone app....and usually fall asleep during the 2nd period!

Robert Campbell
Pittsburgh, USA (now Uppsala, Sweden)
Pittsburgh Penguins

All us European based NHL fans understand the pain that has to be endured in order to listen to or watch our favourite team - staying up until the small hours, going to be early and setting your alarm for a midnight (or worse) get up, staggering into work or school having barely slept - we've all been there. This pain is of course doubled when it comes round to the Play-offs. (For the Leafs fans reading this, the Play-offs are what happens when your guys have packed up and gone home.) My first experience of Play-off hockey came at the end of my first season as a Pittsburgh fan. Christmas 2000 had seen the Penguins receive a late present when Mario Lemieux came out of the retirement to re-join his then struggling team. His arrival sparked a revival in the team's fortunes and they went on to make the post season. Sadly the internet was still in its infancy for me and with edited highlights only on Channel 5 a day or so after the games were played, I relied heavily on Ceefax to keep up to date the Pens' progress and eventual loss to New Jersey in the Eastern Conference Final. Obviously us Pens fans were then starved of Play-off hockey until 2007, but it wasn't until the following season that I truly found out what a deep run in the post season could do to you. With my wife heavily pregnant with our second child, and with the arrival of NASN - and therefore live games on TV, I found myself adjusting my normal day to accommodate the growing number of games that the Pens played. Deeper and deeper they went, more and more I began living off coffee and Red Bull, closer and closer we got to our due date. My Play-off beard grew more and more - I'm using the term 'beard' loosely here - so much so that my almost 2-year-old son wouldn't go near me. Having despatched the Flyers in the Eastern Conference Finals, the Pens went into the Stanley Cup Finals. Unfortunately the Pens went behind early on in the series and faced uphill battle to hang in there. On the night of game 5 I had to go to bed early as I had an important meeting to attend the following morning. So having recorded the game and I came downstairs around 5am to watch the game before heading off to work slightly refreshed. Bizarrely my Sky+ box was still recording something - I should have guessed, but mistakenly I put the TV on with NASN still on and to my surprise the game was still going. In an attempt to find out why I started to watch the recording but ended up ditching it to watch the live broadcast. After Petr Sykora scored the game winner I went back to watching the rest of the game only to then realise I was almost an hour late for work. Sadly it of course didn't work out for the Pens in 2008 and having lost in game 6, and still incredibly groggy from too many sleepless nights, and way too much coffee and Red Bull, one day later my wife went into labour. The whole thing was a blur! Fast-forward one year and, of course, the Pens make the Play-offs again. As one of the favourites, despite their poor regular season showing, I was expecting another deep run. But just as the Play-offs were about to start we were all put on notice of redundancy at work. Despite the axe looming large, I immersed myself in the Play-offs, adopting the routines I'd honed the year before. So when I should have been keeping my nose clean at work and being a model employee I was instead sporting another terrible Play-off beard and staggering around half asleep or yawning my way through meetings. By the time Pittsburgh reached the Final I was actually beginning to want them to win the Cup over me keeping my job! After that amazing game 7, I pulled myself together and thankfully kept my job. I wasn't sure whether my scruffy look and dazed state had been noted, but I was relieved that it hadn't ultimately had an effect. That would have been one hell of a sacrifice - my job over a Stanley Cup!

Rob Howe
Sheffield, England
Pittsburgh Penguins

Some would call it a sacrifice, others devotion but staying up through the night, every night or every other night, 82 times in a year requires a level of commitment not present in fans of other sports. 7 years of sleepless nights seems to bring it to another level but I am going to chose my trip to Pittsburgh in Feb 2012 to see the New York Rangers take on the Pittsburgh Penguins at the Console Energy Centre. Modern times make it easier to travel half way round the world to follow your team but thinking about it and actually doing it are poles apart. Sitting above centre ice as the Pens pull out a 2-0 win, the beginning of their season best 11 game winning streak,

Ice Hockey Nights in Europe

will be my most memorable moment no matter how many more games I attend (and there will be more).

Rob Aherne
Stafford, England
Pittsburgh Penguins

Simple – time and money!!! Game-worn jerseys, merchandise (luckily I have a friend in San Jose), trips to California and, yes, many a time I have stayed awake until 3.30am UK time for playoff games, only getting to sleep at 6am+ (or no sleep at all if it's work the next day!). We've all been there hockey fans…!

Jason Dunn
Woking, England
San Jose Sharks

I changed my life for hockey! I transferred to work permanent nights so I could keep track of the various games that the Blues were playing. I've spent £££ buying jerseys, t-shirts, memorabilia, all direct from the USA, with all their shipping and customs prices. I've worked 7 nights in a row, just to have a night off to watch us play a meaningless late season game against Calgary.

Grant Sales
High Wycombe, England
St Louis Blues

With the time zone issues, then having to stay up till about 4am to watch the games probably counts. I do that regularly on Friday and Saturday nights – it's much more difficult during the week when I have to get up for work, however, if it's game against a division rival...then I will either try and take the following day off work or simply stay up anyway and figure I can catch up on sleep over the next few nights instead. I also postponed a US holiday to California until the Blues played in LA and Anaheim in order to watch them live – although in that case it was probably the friends I stayed with who made the sacrifices!

Sandra Pascoe
Penzance, England
St Louis Blues

Jonathan Northall

My biggest sacrifice as a Lightning fan aside from the obvious staying up until 3/4 am for games, and during the 2004 Stanley Cup run, staying up for a few of the double overtime games, I remember game 6 of the finals in Calgary being up until 5am and then having a GCSE exam the same morning. I'd also have to say my playoff beard from our run to the Conference finals, no one understood why I had this Amish looking beard, friends, family and work mates all questioned its point, but I felt as I kept coming into work/seeing my friends they all got on the Lightning bandwagon by knowing we were still in the playoffs, some where even looking up results to see if the beard would stay.
I think a small part of Bristol was converted to the Lightning thanks to it!

Nathan Cartmel
Bristol, England (now Tampa, FL, USA)
Tampa Bay Lightning

If you will describe it as a sacrifice to fly 10 hours into Florida, to view Alligators or enjoy the beaches around the bay during the day, then that's the largest sacrifice which we have to deliver before enjoying a game at the Forum. But honestly, the only sacrifice is, that we are not able to view some more games!

Alexander, Daniela & Marek Neumann
Schwäbisch Hall, Germany
Tampa Bay Lightning

It is somewhat a given that as a fan who lives in the Czech Republic it is my sleep that I most often sacrifice. Being 6 hours ahead of the East Coast most of the games start around 1:30 in the morning for me and if the Lightning play on the West Coast it can be at 4 or 4:30am. Because of that I sometimes get only 3 or so hours of sleep. But I'm usually more than happy to give up on sleep for my favourite team.
Also, I was lucky enough to visit Tampa myself. I went to 8 games in total (2 in 2011, 6 in 2012) and it was the best time I ever had.

Katerina Brzonova
Zlin, Czech Republic
Tampa Bay Lightning

Biggest sacrifice and most committed hmmm, biggest sacrifice was for years not being able to watch all my teams games in the late 80's to late 90's, I was coming to the UK on and off with family vacations and then finally deciding to live in the UK, but then some of the biggest commitments would before the likes of Sky Sports, Channel 5, NASN, ESPN etc. my family back in Canada would be sending a few games over each month on VHS and press clipping from papers across the pond and I'll be sending the watched ones back for more. Whilst I missed quite a few games, I was happy to be able to watch some of my teams games and keep in touch with the teams goings on, soon as I heard NASN was available I snapped it up right away no matter what the cost was, then the same with ESPN on TV and ESPN Player I subscribed to both and life was restored could watch all the games even what would be pay per view back home so I could watch more hockey in the UK than I could in Canada, also flying home on visits to watch some games is usually always on the cards each season but a lot of that was work permitting though.

AJ
Not disclosed
Toronto Maple Leafs

I'd have to say actually going out to Toronto for the reason of going to games. The cost involved was high, but something that I wanted to do after my first visit. I guess travelling that far for a game has to be committed, and a sacrifice as I was away from my wife for a week

Richard Trowbridge
Cheltenham, England
Toronto Maple Leafs

My biggest sacrifice as a fan is sleep, as 3 to 4 times a week I'm staying up to all hours of the night to watch my Toronto Maple Leafs play. Especially when they are playing on the road against a Western team, where games starts at 2-3am UK time. My most committed act would be flying out to watch opening night game every season in October.
To those who don't understand, a 3,500-mile flight just to watch ice hockey would seem a little insane!

Mark Rackham
Kent, England
Toronto Maple Leafs

After watching the Leafs get hammered 6-2 by the Habs at the Air Canada Centre in April 2009, having already been eliminated from post-season play offs contention (as usual!), I persisted with the plan in New York and took my brother and two friends to New Jersey to see the Leafs again - faith repaid, we won 4-1!

Jonathan Northall

A rather enjoyable drunken night in the end!

Jamie Mash
Northallerton, England
Toronto Maple Leafs

My biggest commitment to watching hockey was probably in Afghanistan in recent years while on a few tours, I managed to grab a few games on TV at Kandahar Airbase and in Camp Bastion.
I gatecrashed the Canadian areas (I was in the British army) as I heard they were watching some Leafs hockey. I never leave home without at least one of my Leafs jerseys so came dressed for the occasion with a Leafs jersey over my uniform, so I managed to watch some NHL games on TV that were beamed in from Canada and recorded for a more suitable time to view the next day. I also managed to play some ball hockey too on the rink in Kandahar and watch some games being played and, on occasion, not even the sirens going off for possible incoming direct fire. Being so far from home, it felt like being back home as I felt like I was amongst friends even though I didn't know them. Being in the British army, its all football and rugby so this was a welcome break for me, it was quite surreal watching NHL on TV and playing ball hockey in Afghanistan.
Whilst the likes of Don Cherry, Tiger Williams, NHL and Maple Leafs Alumni etc. would make visits to the Canadian forces as a morale boost, being in the British army I wasn't aware of such visits for other coalition forces at the time, however on one occasion while walking back from a meeting or such like I found myself doing a double take as I saw some commotion ahead and mass of people walking my way and Don Cherry walked past with his entourage of reporters and Canadian Forces PR guys.
I just shouted "Hi Don!" and gave him a salute out of respect as we walked past one another. In typical Don fashion, I got a thumbs up in return.

Anonymous
Not given
Toronto Maple Leafs

I guess my biggest sacrifice is the same as anyone watching from this side of the pond... staying up until all hours or getting up in the middle of the night to watch games.

Ice Hockey Nights in Europe

This season I've had to watch on my computer too, hopefully by next year I'll be back to checking out games on TV, all being equal!

Matt Merritt
Portsmouth, England
Toronto Maple Leafs

Biggest sacrifice - I guess saving up all my pocket money to use as spending money for my Canadian hockey watching trips. I didn't have a job at that age so my Dad used to pay for the flights and hotel. I have been to Toronto twice and also to Vancouver once and seen the Canucks play. I also regularly watched late night live games on NHL Gamecenter, although limiting midweek viewing due to early work start times.

Tony Harrison
Rutland, England
Toronto Maple Leafs

Losing sleep to watch NHL goes with the territory of "hockey fan". My biggest sacrifice is the amount of money I paid a scalper for my first Toronto game. 13 years later, my wife still doesn't know (and I dare not admit) how much it cost for a pair of tickets to see Leafs-Canadiens in the ACC for my 40th birthday.

Elliott Hall
Sheffield, England
Toronto Maple Leafs

With the time difference between Denmark and the various parts of North America, watching the games live is just that. I guess it's the same for most European fans, though I haven't heard about many other European girls doing it. On weekdays, I usually head to bed around 8pm, since the games starts at 1am. Hopefully I get to sleep the full 5 hours, then watch the game or games and head to work early. Other nights I only get a couple hours of sleep, and sleep a couple of hours after the game. This means I am in a constant lack of sleep throughout the regular season. Watching the game on-demand they next day, just isn't the same! Games in the weekends are easier, but it's all about planning. Gotta be home at 1am. Gotta stay awake. Gotta not get too drunk. Sometimes it's nice with the excuse too, though most look at me, like I'm from another planet, when I tell them: "gotta go, got a game to watch". So far I've been "lucky" that my teams haven't made it to the playoffs. Both ending at the bottom of the Eastern Conference, in the two seasons I've been watching hockey. I can't wait for that to change, and I'm sure it will change soon. And I will gladly give up my beauty sleep to watch my boys get a big win, or just play a game.

Kristina Stryhn Laursen
Copenhagen, Denmark
Toronto Maple Leafs / New York Islanders

I'm betting every fan from Europe will tell you this: waking up 4am or staying up in the middle of the night, to watch a game. If you're a student or a teen, that's probably just fun, but we're often working people, with families and duties. Waking up many nights a season, splitting your bedtime in half just to watch a game is a big sacrifice. My most committed act? Watching every Canucks playoffs game live and then going to work early on.

Michał Pręgowski
Warsaw, Poland
Vancouver Canucks

Haven't really made any big sacrifices but I like to think I'm pretty committed to the Caps. I stay up late for every game of the season to watch on Gamecenter Live rather than watching the replay the next day. It's messed my sleeping patterns up and I've had to start taking naps in the afternoons but I think it's worth it!

Hana Imiolczyk
Merthyr Tydfil, Wales
Washington Capitals

As you said, there's the time difference, I have to go to bed at around 7pm so I can get up at night, usually around 1 or 2am. If I don't have to get up the other day I don't go to bed at all... but that's no problem for me, I'm kind of a night person and I can go for a few days without sleep.... as I think about it, I've never really done anything properly crazy for the team... that's disappointing. I once got to school really late because the game started late and I just couldn't leave. Usually I have to go to school just an hour or so after the game and if it is a particularly good one or a particularly bad one I can't really concentrate on a lesson or an exam...I got a couple of bad grades because of that. No regrets though.

Štěpánka Černá
Dolní Němčí, Czech Republic
Winnipeg Jets

6 IF YOU WERE COMMISSIONER, WHAT ONE THING WOULD YOU CHANGE ABOUT THE NHL?

No matter how I worded the question, I always felt that hockey fans would read this as "please describe how Gary Bettman is incompetent and what is glaringly obvious but he's too stubborn to implement." I was not disappointed. Whatever your feelings are for Commissioner Bettman, I was looking for the fans perspective on what they would change. However, Mr Bettman doesn't get a good deal from this chapter.

From the objective views, European fans do unsurprisingly want more interaction and access to the National Hockey League. The European broadcasting deal debacle from the 2011-12 season is still the source of fan's rancour. For North American fans who aren't aware, TV deals in Europe took far longer to be decided and the season started with some countries still not having coverage. The UK, for example, suffered as a result because coverage disappeared from terrestrial television completely and a small broadcaster won the rights and drove the coverage completely on to pay-per-view to an audience of very few.

The lack of games physically taking place in Europe is also irksome to many. The NHL Premiere series were well received and appreciated but the NHL's current strategy seems to be moving away to outdoor games. The cost of seeing games for fans is prohibitive to many and European games had reduced this burden.

At the time of asking the question, the concept of league alignment was still very much up for debate and fans took the opportunity to put their steer on how they would like to see the league. Interestingly, there are many suggestions to changes to the franchises: moving existing ones and adding new ones. The relocation of the Atlanta Thrashers to Winnipeg has conjured up questions regarding the history of clubs and their reincarnations.

If I were NHL Commissioner I think before a change of ownership in a franchise, relocation or expansion, I'd make sure the location was truly a viable hockey market. I'd do proper due diligence on the prospective new owners so we aren't left with the mistakes that happened in Phoenix, Atlanta and Nashville in recent years of bad ownership or locations. In regards to Phoenix, I would of sold them off to True North (the Winnipeg franchise) as Phoenix were already in NHL ownership and in need of a buyer before Atlanta, then I'd take on the ownership of Atlanta until a new buyer was found for them. The reason why I say this is because I hate there being two different franchises sharing the same name as we do now not just with the Ottawa Senators but now also with the Winnipeg Jets, this is partly due to some fans thinking their new team has links to the other franchise when in fact it doesn't share anything in common except for a name, as such the NHL missed out on a great opportunity in my opinion to relocate the exact same team back to Winnipeg where it first moved from, thus the modern Jets would indeed be the same franchise as the Phoenix / Jets franchise and could continue with the same heritage.

AJ
Not disclosed
Toronto Maple Leafs

Given the serious backward step that NHL broadcasting rights have taken in the UK, I feel that would be the biggest priority moving forward. The NHL clearly has a desire to improve the league's standing in Europe. The Premiere games are a great foundation and they were something I thoroughly enjoyed watching in-person this season, but the TV rights situation is the first thing that needs addressing if the league is to increase its footprint in Europe.
They need to be a viable, affordable option for as many people as possible.

Alex Nunn
Romford, England
New York Rangers

As a Commissioner, I have a lot of stuff to consider within the league itself like CBA negotiations and conference adjustments.
From the perspective of a European, I have two issues:
At first I would implement a "Game of the Day" every Saturday and Sunday which should be scheduled at 2pm Eastern to match the 8pm spot in Central Europe and sell these games to European broadcasters.
In my mind that would force a lot of broadcasters to bid for the rights and may be result in a larger interest in the NHL.

2nd: I would build up a partnership, likely with Amazon, to sell merchandising in Europe without the actual tax problems because it's really frustrating to buy from nhl.com, get a shipping from U.S. and cannot calculate the final payment because of the import taxes which German customs calculate for a product which was previously imported from China into the U.S.

Alexander, Daniela & Marek Neumann
Schwäbisch Hall, Germany
Tampa Bay Lightning

On a personal note - I'd ban the term 'Smashville' makes my skin crawl every time I hear it hollered by Preds fans, or splattered all over their marketing. I'd also make the phrases 'Upper/Lower body injury' outlawed – please tell us actually what is going on with our players, and when we may see them again! I don't believe really in tinkering with the rules of the game, however potentially I would change the overtime/Shoot-out points award. I feel it gives too much incentive for defensive teams and doesn't reward teams that genuinely try to win in regulation. The two points for a win system also causes bunching, and less of a distinction for genuinely good teams. It is almost as if the NHL want the teams to be bunch, by not rewarding trying to win. I'd give 3 points for a win in regulation, 2 points for OT/SO win, 1 point for OT or SO loss. Also – abolish the winners of divisions seeded top 3, absolutely ridiculous. Fine if they automatically qualify for the playoffs, just seed them where they finish – 1st to 8th.

Allan Allison
Bristol, England
Anaheim Ducks

More games starting at midday or early afternoon so I wouldn't need to miss too much sleep as the games would then start in the early evening instead of 12 at night in the UK.

Amy Hill
Camberley, England
Boston Bruins

Make sure the game gets more coverage in the UK. Channel 5's coverage was excellent, but unless you have an obscure satellite channel, you have to rely on the website. Other than that, I would like to see more expansion teams go to Canada.
Winnipeg had a good first season but there's other major hockey markets

like Quebec and Victoria, which should be exploited.

Andy Parsons
London, England
Colorado Avalanche

Should increase the penalties for hits to the head.

Bartek Pexu
Warsaw, Poland
Boston Bruins

I would like to see the end of the shootout to decide games and move to continuous 3 on 3 OT. It will really open up the ice and keeps the victory (or defeat) a complete team effort. I really don't like the shootout to decide games and it needs to end.

Bradley Marsh
Essex, England
Detroit Red Wings

It's so hard to choose ONE thing. I guess the most pressing would be hits to the head. No fine. No suspension. Just an outright ban for the offending player. As a commissioner, you have to realise that making money is significant for any league of any sport but it's nowhere near as important as player safety. Just recently there have been so many concussion-related injuries throughout the league its becoming quite tricky keeping track. Marc Savard and Sidney Crosby are amongst the high profile names to have suffered recently from something which - contact sport or not - there is no good reason for. Another thing I'd love to see - perhaps as part of the NHL Premiere set up (where some teams play their opening couple of games in Europe) - is the winner of the annual NHL All-Star game playing a different European champion each season. It's asking a lot where travel is concerned and fatigue's a huge issue as it is but just imagine the All-Stars playing a team nobody's ever heard of from Britain, Sweden, Russia... wherever. That's my referendum. Mr Bettman, I'll expect your call....

Chris Bluff
Stockton-On-Tees, England
Dallas Stars

If I were NHL Commissioner, I would change the NHL schedule to create a better schedule with more games between east and west teams. As a

Ice Hockey Nights in Europe

Canuck, I would love to see more games against teams such as Toronto, Montreal and Boston. I would alter the play off system also to make it possible that you could have an East versus East final or West versus West final. I'm a believer in the Stanley Cup Finals being between the two best teams.

Dan Birkin
Burton upon Trent, England
Vancouver Canucks

If I were the Commissioner of the NHL, the one thing I would change is the disciplinary process. More specifically having a third party person acting as the chief of discipline. I think that Brendan Shanahan has done a better job than Colin Campbell, but I think that he has not been consistent enough in his decision-making. Too many times he has refused to discipline a so-called "star" player even though it is obvious that they should have been disciplined. Shea Weber's actions against Henrik Zetterberg were the latest example of this. I think a third party disciplinarian would be good for the league as they would provide some more consistency and actually be a lot stricter with some of the more dirty plays.

Daruish Gorgirzadeh
Bournemouth, England
New York Rangers

If I were commissioner of the NHL, I would scrap the shootout and increase overtime to 10 minutes with 5 minutes being 4 on 4 and the other half 3 on 3. That would make interesting hockey. If neither team wins the game after overtime, then it is ruled a tie. There is nothing wrong with an old fashioned tie! With regards to relocation, I would move Phoenix to Quebec City to bring back the Nordiques. Canada needs another team. I would move Columbus to Seattle. Seattle is a fantastic city that could potentially create a rivalry with Vancouver and definitely has the size to support an NHL team. I would also pitch an idea to a US network to build a US equivalent of 'Hockey Night in Canada' with no guesses as to what it would be called! Creating double headers for one night a week would be advantageous for the 'brand'. It is a shame that ESPN does not like hockey because they did a good job with televising the sport a few years ago.

David Lidbury
Bristol, England
Philadelphia Flyers

Jonathan Northall

I would not support hockey market like for example is Phoenix now. I would support more Canadians teams in the league. I also would focus more on European fans – more attractive game times on the weekends, one big European fan club organizing trips to the North America and more.

David Púchovský
Bratislava, Slovakia
Colorado Avalanche

I'd probably try to enforce stricter rules against obstructions and even though the league has improved over the course of last season with Brendan Shanahan in charge, it also needs more consistent league discipline and suspension rulings. It's good that all suspensions are explained through a short video but what's missing are the same kind of videos for controversial scenes that didn't result in a suspension. When you see multiple players from your team getting concussed during the season (Miller, Gerbe, or Kaleta who got sucker-punched and injured by Gauthier some seasons ago but the scene went largely unnoticed and Kaleta has battled neck-injuries ever since) by hits that were deemed illegal by the on-ice-officials but then there is no further league discipline and, in Grebe's case, not even a real explanation why there wasn't, it's very frustrating.

David Trippler
Mainz, Germany
Buffalo Sabres

I would expand the NHL to a 4 division, 32-team league and try to improve the balance of Canadian teams to American, reintroducing the Nordiques to the NHL as well as giving Hamilton an NHL franchise. Getting the NHL out of Phoenix would be my second job.

Diarmuid Murray
Dublin, Rep of Ireland
Montreal Canadiens

I'd get rid of the draft lottery. It's crazy! If you finish 30th in the league you should have the pick of the best college players around. That is the best way to ensure parity. Other than that I would keep the game pretty much as it is.

Ed Johnston
Somerset, England
New York Rangers

Ice Hockey Nights in Europe

Should I change only one thing? Oh no! There are many things I would change…Ok, as I have told many times, the first thing I would change is the shootout, that's to say it's suppression: I hate shootout to determine the winner of a game. I have always hated the shootout even when I was a kid and only followed football (I'm European and won't use the word "soccer"). I don't like the winner of a game to be determined by a "lottery". So, please come back to the old rule: no winner after the OT? Tied game!

Emanuela Pozzi
Cernusco sul Naviglio, Italy
New Jersey Devils

For me this has to be UK / European merchandising, to get stuff sent here from the States costs an absolute fortune especially after import tax. I feel if they had some kind of European based warehouse to supply Europe keeping the costs down a lot more merchandise would be bought across Europe, I know I'd buy loads! Every other sport from across the pond seems to have jerseys and other merchandise readily available in sports shops, especially the NFL and NBA. All I have seen from the NHL over here is a few caps and they never had Devils caps! As for the sport itself leave it ALONE! Don't fix what don't need fixing; the NHL game is perfect as it is stop trying to change it!

Gavin Clarke
Bristol, England
New Jersey Devils

In terms of the on-ice action I don't think there is a lot to change. The NHL is a great league and continues to attract and thrill a lot of fans on a yearly basis. They tried to alter the league structure, which was an unnecessary move in my opinion and was correctly rejected. Along with a lot of fellow European fans, I would change the international coverage of the NHL. I think the league is a bit narrow minded at times, and feels their support is only from Canada and the States, forgetting that a large part of the leagues players and supporters are from Europe. In comparison to the NFL, the coverage we get here in England is pretty shoddy at best. We get a few games a week on a channel that has been given a lot of criticism regarding their coverage. In addition, to get this channel you have to pay extra money on top of the usual sports package, which works out at a pretty steep rate each month. I think GameCenter Live is a phenomenal piece of technology and really helps out a lot of fans outside of America and

Canada. However, if I were Mr Bettman, my number one priority would be to sort out the television coverage in Europe. It will only help spread and develop the amazing game.

George Royle
Malmesbury, England
Dallas Stars

From a "European NHL fan" perspective, top priority is sorting out the broadcasting rights for UK/Europe. As proven, the NHL has a large and dedicated following outside North America. A large number of which go to extremes (and possibly technically illegal means) to follow their team.

Gord Turner
Manchester, England
Toronto Maple Leafs

I'd revamp the referee's structure. Have them made accountable for blown calls, inconsistent refereeing and plain incompetence. I understand the game is fast, but there are too many bad calls going unpunished or seen to be favouring one team over another.

Grant Sales
High Wycombe, England
St Louis Blues

This may be a really superficial thing to want to change but since I've never had problems watching the games, I'd open a UK or EU online store for the NHL. It's really difficult to get the official merchandise over here without paying huge custom bills on its arrival. I know many people probably resort to buying their jerseys from eBay where they are normally counterfeits just because it's much cheaper to do. But beyond the jerseys it's really hard to get T-shirts, pucks, hoodies etc.!

James Bird
Burnley, England
Pittsburgh Penguins

As a European NHL fan, I think my answer will be one, which I'm sure many will agree with, NHL on free view TV. Now I am being realistic with this and I know free view channels here in the UK like BBC and ITV wouldn't fork out much money for the TV rights so the NHL wont get much income BUT I feel that the Playoffs should be broadcast on free view and then, if this is a success then perhaps the bigger companies like Sky can take on the regular season rights for the NHL. So if I were commissioner, I would open talks with European TV companies!!!!!

James Cartwright
Cardiff, Wales
New York Islanders

I'd begin with sending the TV rights out to more nations. Obviously, I'm biased in answering that as a Brit, but if he wants the NHL to gain even more international awareness and interest then that's the step to take. There's no point in bringing NHL Season Premiere games to countries that don't get to see much of the NHL otherwise because there will be less interest. I'm sure it might be a sell-out if the Season Premiere did return to the UK, but imagine how much more that could grow if only there were better TV rights here. The NHL makes enough money already to not need to worry quite as much about the value of international rights, so why not just start them off at a cheaper rate, and then when interest picks up, hike up the prices as channels fight for the TV rights. It has worked wonders for the NFL. The only thing that stands in the way of this is the late start time of games. Although weekend match ups could still be realistically shown at a fair hour.

James Willis
Watford, England
New York Rangers

The schedule – regular season could be shorter, make all teams play each other at least once, make playoffs even longer! EVERYONE prefers playoff hockey.

Jason Dunn
Woking, England
San Jose Sharks

I would immediately get rid of touch icing - too many injuries for this to be viable.

Joan Chisholm
Washington, England
Edmonton Oilers

Jonathan Northall

This one was a hard one to choose, between moving teams that are struggling to make money to better, more hockey-friendly markets, quicker, and making sure that the whole of Europe got a better TV deal, to allow the sport to gain a larger worldwide fan base. Really, I would like to do both of those things, but the most logical one to do first, if I were commissioner, would be the first option I mentioned. The Phoenix Coyotes, particularly, I would look to move into a place like Seattle, as quickly as possible, where the team has a better chance of surviving and thriving.
Perhaps, as an extension of this movement, I would also add two more expansion franchises (Mostly likely Quebec, and either Toronto or Kansas City) to help keep the divisions more equal.

Joe Alderson
Stoke-on-Trent, England
Detroit Red Wings

I would make the concussions rule much more tight which stop players coming back so quickly and maybe a specialist on each bench this way the best ways will be 100% healthy and can play for a longer period of time not losing star players so early because of concussions.

Junaid Hussain
Nottingham, England
Detroit Red Wings

The most discussed topic has been the player safety.
With the number of head injuries happening to players all around the league (affecting the star players as well) I wish there was a big change in this matter. I've read many articles about this issue and I know it won't be a matter of one season; it is a very complex problem. I would start with very strict and harsh punishments for illegal hits to the players' heads. I would also get rid off the reasoning that is nowadays used in order to justify shorter suspensions – star player status, elimination or playoff game. That all should not matter at all in making a decision about suspension.
I would also like a much more strict system which would prevent players from hiding their head injuries (concussions). It's one thing to play through a broken bone, it's a completely different situation with "broken brain". Players need to be taught that it is okay to report a head injury and that it is completely not okay to try playing through it.

Though, this is not up to the league, it's more so about the policy and philosophy of every single team.

Katerina Brzonova
Zlin, Czech Republic
Tampa Bay Lightning

I would like to see a change to the points system to a fairer and more reflective structure of 3, 2, 1: 3 points for a regulation win, 2 for an overtime/shootout win and 1 for a an overtime loss. I believe that other leagues around the world would take their lead from the NHL and that it would be a fairer system for everybody as it rewards teams who are able to win within 60 minutes, recognising the ability of a team to get the job done – simply put, a shootout win should not be seen to be as valuable as a regulation win – it's a question of common sense and I for one hope the NHL see fit to update these rules.

Katy Parles
Newcastle Upon Tyne, England
Calgary Flames

I'd try and bring in more teams into Canada, it's almost a tragedy that there are (at the moment) 7 Canadian teams and we all know that a city or two can profit from an NHL franchise, Quebec's been in the pipeline and it'd be nice to see an 8th team reside there. It's Canada's sport, thus more teams, but I wouldn't relocate a team unless it really had to come to it (i.e. Atlanta-Winnipeg). There'd be more options, but you only want one.

Kenny Jones
Caernarfon, Wales
LA Kings

Consistency when it comes to bans and punishment. The amount of stuff that guys can get away with purely as they are "star" players is disgusting. Case in point, Weber smashing Zetterberg's head into the glass twice, only received a $2500 fine, if Lucic had done that, it would have been an instant ban. The rules need to be enforced against EVERY player, and they need to be consistent. Marchand received 5 games for clipping Salo, whilst the Canucks that jumped Thornton to the ground get nothing.

Jonathan Northall

A Canuck also clipped Lucic, received nothing.

Kimmi Noble
Sheffield, England
Boston Bruins

I would make the game more accessible to everyone if I were Commissioner of the NHL. Even fans in North America suffer with poor coverage with some games "blacked out" due to NHL restrictions in only allowing games to broadcast in local regions. Fans across the rest of the world have limited or restricted television coverage and although there are now Internet packages, that is only ok if you have a fast enough broadband connection. To promote the game we love it needs to be accessible to as many people as possible on every format.

Mark Rackham
Kent, England
Toronto Maple Leafs

Hmmmm, tough question, I think the NHL does a pretty good job of it at the moment. I would love to see more NHL games in Europe but this means less played in North America so isn't really a goer. Given all that went on with the confusion over the NHL TV deal for Europe, a more coherent approach to overseas TV would be ideal. I would also change the draft, at the moment there is a lottery for the number one pick, I would do away with that. I would stick with the top 30 pick's being decided by the NHL final season standings. So: 30th ranked team gets the number 1 pick 29th ranked team gets the number 2 pick etc. So there are a few little things I would change not any one big thing. The NHL is pretty good at the moment, it just needs tweaking!

Mark Woodcock
Macclesfield, England
Phoenix Coyotes

Though I'm not so interested in the business around the NHL this question is quite tricky. The first thing that appears in my head is to change the points system. Today, you can get a maximum 2 points per game. No matter if you win in regulation or by penalty shootout. I think that kind of system affects the league in a negative way though the teams that play a defensive kind of hockey can take the game to a draw and later earn 2 points in the shoot out. In my opinion, you have to reward an offensive way of playing in order to get larger crowds and by that a higher income. In

Sweden, you get 3 points for a win in regulation, 2 points for an overtime win and 1 point for a overtime loss. If the NHL would use this system it would give the teams that want to play a crowd-friendly and offensive hockey an advantage. We would also see bigger and faster changes in the standings. As it is today, it is very hard to climb the table just because you don't gain anything by a regulation win compared to an overtime win. Consider a scenario where two teams are struggling to make the post-season. There are 2 points between them. By getting three points by winning in regulation I think the trailing team would go for it and pass the opponent in the standings instead of playing safe and relying on the shoot-out where they get 2 points by winning and the losing team gets 1. And where they still will be behind in the standings.

Mattias Boström
Stockholm, Sweden
Colorado Avalanche

If I were commissioner I would ensure that the NHL had full control over it's own TV rights to provide the world full coverage of the world's best sporting league. Roughly 30% of the NHL is made up of European players, we should be allowed to express our support equally! Instead many of us are restricted to watching Internet streams and the occasional handful of games per week through an unreliable TV broadcaster.

Melanie Warn
Devon, England
Calgary Flames

The big talk right now, and for a good reason, is lack of consistency in suspension handling. The Player Safety team has to come up with clear rules - and enforce these rules without hesitation. By all means stop that sentence-based-on-effect nonsense. It's the intent to hurt the other player that has to be eradicated. I'm not sure if Brendan Shanahan is up to it. He started on a high note but, after the Weber-Zetterberg incident, he's losing credibility. When players like Zetterberg and Henrik Sedin, who are generally very clean, feel the need to retaliate for nasty hits by rivals, you know you have a problem. NHL, wake up before someone gets seriously hurt and many people decide to stop watching hockey.

Michał Pręgowski
Warsaw, Poland
Vancouver Canucks

Jonathan Northall

I think I'd get rid of the draft lottery system, if you finish bottom of the league you deserve the first pick. For me, it is hugely frustrating to see a team leap up the order to select a potential franchise player, like the Devils did with Adam Larsson. It's even worse however when it gives the lottery winner the opportunity to pick first especially for fans of that bottom team. There have been some very significant instances of that as well, the Penguins should have had the chance to draft Ovechkin but were denied it by Washington getting lucky, not that I feel too sorry for them getting Malkin but it's not often that there are two players like that available. Simply put, I see no need to have the lottery in place.

Mike Fuller
Newcastle, England
Colorado Avalanche

Don't get me started on this. There are many things that need addressing but my main ones would probably have to be referee accountability and the implementation of a consistent disciplinary system. There is also the points system to consider. Do away with the loser point, no three-point games. There is also the "tanking aspect". Rewarding a team for consistent failure by having the first overall pick or a top three pick a couple of years in a row masks GM incompetence and rewards losing. Why not do this - make it impossible for a team that had the top pick the previous year to have that pick the following year? Give them a chance to pick in the top five, but remove them from the top pick lottery by default. Also, if a team picked in the top three two years in a row, make it impossible for them to do so for the third consecutive year.

Mislav Jantoljak
Zagreb, Croatia
Pittsburgh Penguins / Toronto Maple Leafs

If I was Mr Bettman, the first thing I would do is get rid of the shootout. Too many teams getting an extra point for a skills competition, and a win or a loss by a shootout for me can never really be classed as either. I feel North American fans need to understand that a draw is ok, and if two teams are tied after a full 60 minutes and 5 minutes of 4 on 4 then a point each is just fine.

Nathan Cartmel
Bristol, England (now Tampa, FL, USA)
Tampa Bay Lightning

Yes the trapezoid can go, Division winners should only be guaranteed playoff spots not the top 3 seeds & realignment needs to happen, but if I were the commissioner of the NHL, I would get rid of the shootout. It's just an infuriatingly stupid way of ending a game. What was wrong with ties anyway? The NFL, the biggest league in North America has ties, why can't the NHL? It's just another major reason as to way the playoffs are the greatest time of year, as there are no shootouts.

One of my favourite playoff games that I watched was the 5OT Keith Primeau overtime game against the Pens. Obviously this is not workable during regular season play, but people far smarter than me have suggested a 5 minute 4 on 4 period, followed by 5 minutes of 3 on 3 if no team have scored. That would work. The TV companies can have an extra ad break as well. The shootout is also partly responsible for the 3-point games the NHL currently allow.

Ray Skeates
Basingstoke, England
Philadelphia Flyers

I'd rearrange the points structure for games and get rid of the shootout. Overtime would be 4 on 4 for 5 minutes then 3 on 3 for 5 minutes. If no-one scores then its a draw. A game shouldn't be decided on a skills exercise. Points wise I'd have 3 points for a win and 1 for a draw. If you lose in overtime its a loss and should be 0 points. If it's a tie game then it's a tie game, simple.
Works well in football over here, and I'd like to see it in the NHL

Richard Trowbridge
Cheltenham, England
Toronto Maple Leafs

It would be nice to think as Commissioner I could change any aspect of the game but the days of omnipotence are long gone with team GM's debating all potential rules changes and voting them in or out. I would, however, put forward the idea of a change to the playoff structure for the second rounds and beyond. It seems fair to guarantee a playoff spot for a team that wins its division but some divisions turn out weaker than others and there can be a difference of 10-15 points between a division winner and a higher scoring 3rd place team in another division.

Playoff seeding should revert to total points scored in the season once the first round of playoffs are completed.

Rob Aherne
Stafford, England
Pittsburgh Penguins

This is another tough question. I'm torn over Gary Bettman. There are some things about him that I like and there are some things I don't like. I appreciate that he's in a difficult spot trying to promote the best interests of a sport - primarily in North America - where it lags behind the NFL, NBA and MLB, but at times he doesn't help himself with some of the bizarre decisions, particularly over TV rights which seem to be an issue no matter whereabouts in the world you are. The one thing I would change about the NHL is the way supplementary discipline is managed and administered - especially where head shots are concerned. For me, the inconsistency with which Brendan Shanahan is currently dealing with this is creating more uncertainty, more confusion and ultimately causing more incidents on the ice. I don't necessarily blame Shanahan completely as I'm almost certain he continues to be influenced by the league and the General Managers. However, when you get different suspensions handed down for what appears to all and sundry to be identical incidents, and star players receiving miniscule suspensions in comparison to known 'goons' something has to be done. If not, the position will only continue because without hard and fast rules - for everyone irrespective of their status as players - confusion will reign.

Rob Howe
Sheffield, England
Pittsburgh Penguins

As a permanent resident of hockey-mad Sweden, I have no complaints about the NHL TV deal here. As a matter of fact, I get to see many more Penguins games in Sweden than I ever did in Los Angeles or San Francisco. There are just a few things I would therefore change if I were Commissioner...and they all at one time were already in place in the NHL. The first would be to eliminate the silly shootouts during the regular season! I never once had an issue with the way hockey games were decided pre-Bettman: a 10 minute overtime with one point to each team if no goals are scored; two points if a team scores; and zero if a team gets scored on. Shootouts to decide the outcome of a game are like deciding a tie baseball game with a homerun hitting contest, and NFL game with a field goal kicking competition, or a basketball game with a free throw challenge.

Ice Hockey Nights in Europe

Absolute insanity! I would also bring back the old division and conference names that made the NHL such a unique league: Prince of Wales & Campbell Conferences and Patrick, Norris, Adams, and Smythe Divisions! Those were the days!

Robert Campbell
Pittsburgh, USA (now Uppsala, Sweden)
Pittsburgh Penguins

If I were the Commissioner of the NHL, the one change I would make would be to promote the NHL in the UK and Europe more. The main focus of this change would be television coverage that is widely available, maybe even an NHL network on UK television with multiple channels that showed most games, the league really needs to provide abetter service for its European fan base!

Robert Weaver
Gloucestershire, England
Ottawa Senators

If I were Commissioner of the NHL I would make it more accessible for people to watch globally, I would have more games played in other parts of Europe, not just in Scandinavia and I would also move the likes of Florida and Phoenix further north to a city that deserves and appreciates the sport of ice hockey.

Ryan McCue
Glasgow, Scotland
Toronto Maple Leafs

The only thing I would change is the shootouts. I would cancel them and make regular season games just like in the playoffs, adding 20 minutes overtimes until somebody scores. I find it very bothering that a great tied nerve wracking game has to be decided in such a primitive way. Oh and point system. I would make it 3 pts. for a win in regulation, 2 for a win in OT and 1 for a loss in OT.

Štěpánka Černá
Dolní Němčí, Czech Republic
Winnipeg Jets

If I was NHL commissioner, the one thing I would change is that the worst team in the league automatically receives the number one pick in the draft.

Jonathan Northall

Although the NBA uses a similar lottery system, the worst team in the NFL is able to use the number one pick to help rebuild their team. It seems only fair that fans that suffer a dreadful season are rewarded with the prospect of adding a talented young player to their team.

Steve McCaskill
Maidstone, England
Columbus Blue Jackets

Up until this season, the one thing I would have changed is clarity in the disciplinary procedures. This has happened with Brendan Shanahan, and I hope that it will continue. Now I would to change the alignment and the scheduling. I know that this is something being done but I would also look to expand the NHL by two teams; one in Ontario to capitalise on a thriving hockey market and one in the US to attempt to expand the market there. Although careful consideration must be taken to not repeat the mistakes in Atlanta and Phoenix!

Stuart Coles
Coventry, England
LA Kings

If I were Commissioner, my first step would be to remove the instigator penalty. The game can police itself happily. Dirty players know they will get their beatdown on the next shift, but the instigator rule allows players to do what they want, and only have to answer to the ref, not to anyone else. Sometimes the ref doesn't see things, or sees them out of context so punishments/suspensions do not fit with the crime. Without the instigator rule, players control how dirty the game becomes. If someone is playing cheap, then they'll get a punch in the face, or they'll get dirty play straight back at them.

Stuart Wilson
York, England
Detroit Red Wings

If I were commissioner, I'd make the NHL TV rights available to Europe. More viewers equal more fans and thus a new generation of players.

Tim Barnes
Cambridge, England (born in New Jersey, USA)
Philadelphia Flyers

Ice Hockey Nights in Europe

If I were commissioner I would ensure that NHL fans all over the world had access to watch the game. The way the NHL handled the European broadcast rights was disgraceful. With the NFL and the NBA facing uncertain futures, it was a perfect opportunity for the NHL to thrive, but instead they failed and have gone backwards in my opinion. The NHL has many Europeans playing in the league and the European fans have the right to watch those players play in the best league in the world. The NHL Premiere games that have been held in Europe the last few seasons have been a huge hit, with the games selling out in record time. For those fans to not be able to watch the start of the 2011/2012 season and not knowing if they would be able to watch any of it, was a disgraceful way to treat fans that follow the game so passionately.

Tom Harding
Isle of Wight, England
Pittsburgh Penguins

If I were the NHL commissioner I'd have regular NHL games played in Europe and obviously the UK in particular. I think it would be great if maybe 6 games were played in European countries each season although I understand the costs for the NHL and teams involved probably make this difficult.

Tony Harrison
Rutland, England
Toronto Maple Leafs

If I were commissioner of the NHL, the one thing I would change would be to make visors mandatory. It may seem a little excessive when you see pictures/videos of 1970's games and the players skate around with no helmets, but the game is faster, the athletes stronger and the shots are harder. When you see footage of the Bryan Berard injury that shelved his career, you can't help but think 'what if he was wearing a visor?'. I've heard that players who have started using the visor complain about blind spots. This is something that would be an irritant, I get that, but visors have change so much since they were first used, I can't imagine that this problem wouldn't be solved in the not to distant future. Surely player safety should be the number 1 priority of the NHLPA.

Vicki Morgan
Basingstoke, England
Minnesota Wild

Jonathan Northall

7 WHERE DO YOU STAND ON THE FIGHTING DEBATE?

Most questions created diversity of opinion but the fighting debate seems to have much agreement with European hockey fans. Digging behind the reasoning for such agreement, hockey fans then diverge in their opinions. As unusual as it turned out to be, the dissenting voices make some good arguments that would warrant further exploration.

My question on fighting revolves around the message it sends to younger fans. I would argue that fans are desensitized when it comes to fighting. For example, the popular 'NHL' series of games from EA Sports have introduced the option to "drop the gloves". To win the fight, you furiously hammer away at the keys on your controller until someone wins the fight. Compare that to the 'UFC' mixed martial arts series and it somehow looks tame. My point is that it is nonchalantly handled as 'part of the game'.

The biggest talking point revolved around the inforcer / 'goon' mentality. Spontaneity seems to be the key to fans wanting fighting to continue in hockey. A planned 'drop the puck then drop the gloves' approach wears thin on fans. Also, the deaths of Rypien, Boogaard and Belak have brought home the human side of fighting in hockey. Mental health is a serious issue and I can't help but feel that these guys have been victims of a culture akin to the gladiatorial days of Ancient Rome. Perhaps they were failed by am insufficient support network but the pressure to fight game after game must have been immense.

Personally, I think an occasional fight in the context of the game is justified. Perhaps, as others suggest, greater penalties should be meted out but an outright ban made lead to other forms of retribution that are even less desirable. The goalie fight between Brent Johnson and Rick Di Pietro is a fabulous example of spontaneous fighting with the outcome being neither getting hurt. Well, maybe Di Pietro's pride slightly....

To me, fighting is an integral part of the game of hockey, and something I would not want to see removed anytime soon. I can understand people's frustrations with staged fighting, but I do feel it can be something that impacts the momentum of any given game. If there's one problem I do have, it's with fighting after a clean hit. Too often a player is forced to

Ice Hockey Nights in Europe

answer for a picture-perfect play when he shouldn't have to.

Alex Nunn
Romford, England
New York Rangers

Fighting is firmly part of hockey for me. It's a tough sport, and you have to have the opportunity to defend cheap shots and even scores on the ice. If you didn't, more dangerous things could creep in, give angry men sticks without the opportunity to drop gloves and they will use the sticks instead. The current rules are fine; punish one-sided instigators and third men in, however, if two guys drop gloves under their own volition then that's part of hockey. If they choose to do it for the team then that's fine too. The role of the 'goon' is effectively dying, and I'd probably feel stronger against fighting if it wasn't. There are barely any players in the NHL who are there just to punch people, and don't have any other role of the team. Having a 'hard man' is fine, especially if that hard man is someone like Milan Lucic, Niklas Kronwall, or Dion Phaneuf — highly skilled people who just won't take anything if pushed. Physicality is part of hockey, and outlawing fighting is the start of a slippery slope to becoming a non-contact sport.

Allan Allison
Bristol, England
Anaheim Ducks

It's part of the game. Always has been and always will be.

Amy Hill
Camberley, England
Boston Bruins

It is part of the game, keep it in. The NHL has done a good job of getting rid of head hits to their credit. You don't want to see a goon invasion, but the big men get the skilled players to show us what they can do. They need protecting. Plus the fans love it. Take away the fighting, take away the fans.

Andy Parsons
London, England
Colorado Avalanche

Jonathan Northall

Fights are the part of hockey. Is OK as it is now

Bartek Pexu
Warsaw, Poland
Boston Bruins

My personal feelings on the fighting debate are that it is fine in the game at the moment. I know there were a few high profile deaths involving fighters last summer, but before that I don't think it was much thought upon. I understand that it is a risky business and can cause trouble to players in later life, but with the way the NHL game is going nowadays, the onus is being taken away from fighting and enforcers as the game is becoming quicker and many more players are more than just fighters nowadays. I also agree with fighting because it does protect some of the star players because if players know there is no fighting in the game they may start to take liberties and cause more horrible injuries that the NHL can't afford at the moment.

Daruish Gorgirzadeh
Bournemouth, England
New York Rangers

Fighting has been around for years and I lean towards it staying in the game. It is sad when you see a player go hard or awkwardly onto the ice after a fight, fearing he is okay and that is when I feel fighting should not be present. On the other hand, it really is 'part of the game' and I personally feel it will not be taken away in the NHL. In major junior hockey, some figures are calling for fighting to go the way of the NCAA and Olympic ruling where it is banned completely. That is a dangerous mentality because when juniors come into the professional leagues, they are going to find it tough to protect themselves. Fighting has been decreasing in the last 4 years and 2011/12 saw the lowest 'fights per game' in 6 seasons. As long as fighting is kept between 'enforcers' on the ice, I am fine with that. I don't like it when someone of Chara's build targets a Briere type figure.

David Lidbury
Bristol, England
Philadelphia Flyers

I definitely support fights in the hockey. In many cases it could help to add energy for the losing team. It could reverse the whole game. Fights are great shows for hockey fans too. Players would do anything for a win – even lose teeth and bleeding. Enforces and maybe also power forwards are also bodyguards of the biggest stars on the team. Actually, the hockey does not support the classic fighters anymore like, for example, Scott Parker from the Avs or David Koci. The NHL still requires fighters, but also with abilities on the penalty kill at least, and maybe scoring skills.

David Púchovský
Bratislava, Slovakia
Colorado Avalanche

The role of fighting in the NHL is a significant one, in my opinion it is necessary, fans come to see fights in NHL rival games. It somehow adds to the atmosphere of the sport. The main reason however that I feel fighting is necessary is that it helps resolve conflict between two players who have been at each other's throats, I also feel that if fighting was outlawed it would leave many less significant players to go out on the ice with the sole intent of injuring a player leading to teams facing fines and higher suspensions for players and may also lead to more head shots and concussions. The NHL is better with fighting than without it.

Diarmuid Murray
Dublin, Rep of Ireland
Montreal Canadiens

I'm happy for it to play a part of the game within reason. For example, the Penguins versus Flyers matches have been nothing short of disgraceful. There is no need for that. But as part and parcel if you think a team mate has been roughed up then I'm on all for somebody stepping in and dishing out some on-ice justice.

Ed Johnston
Somerset, England
New York Rangers

To me, fighting is an important part of hockey. It can completely flip the momentum of the game. When does the crowd get behind a guy more than when he drops the gloves? The rest of the team does also giving them an extra boost of energy to get out there and perform maybe get that game tying or winning goal. Just by having a goon, or someone the other team knows is handy, dropping the gloves on the ice can make them think twice about getting too physical. If a team is intimidated or, even a certain player on the ice, they're not going to play to their full potential. There is also the protection aspect, if you have one of your star players on the ice and the other team know you have a handy fighter on the bench, their less likely to target him with a big hit risking him an injury as the retaliation could be ending up with a five minute fighting major and a bit of a beating themselves. Another thing is a lot of the more aggressive players who fight a lot are also easily agitated, this means that a player on the opposition roster can wind them up and get them to come after them getting a 5 minute fighting major and possibly drawing an instigator penalty putting their team on the power play. With all this said about the crowd getting behind the team, after a fight on road ice, it can have the opposite effect to your advantage and make the home crowd silent if there guy gets beat down, thus taking away some of the bonus of their home ice advantage. And finally, if you manage to get one of the other teams star players into a fight, you have removed him from the ice for five minutes, and the advantage of doing that is huge. So, all in all, if you remove fighting from the game, you completely change a big part of the game. The NHL is perfect as it is and they need to leave the rules alone.

Gavin Clarke
Bristol, England
New Jersey Devils

I've heard the "Ice Hockey?? That's just fighting on skates, isn't it??" routine from non-fans more times that I'd care to imagine, but I still believe that fighting has its place within the sport. Whilst from an outsider point of view, it can sound/look like "random acts of senseless violence". Any fan will tell you that there is a set system to it that allows the players to "police" themselves to a certain degree.
Hockey is a game that works on momentum, and a fight at the right time (and with the right result) is like a big goal and can be a real game-changer (and as Don Cherry has pointed out on many occasions, if you watch the crowd during a fight, there aren't too many people that aren't on their feet, cheering!)

Gord Turner
Manchester, England
Toronto Maple Leafs

I have no problem with fighting. However, all players who fight should be scanned afterwards, like boxing, to discover more on the problems that lie with concussions and the high rate of mortality amongst enforcers. I would also get rid of the instigator penalty.

Grant Sales
High Wycombe, England
St Louis Blues

Ice Hockey Nights in Europe

Fighting is part of the game. Take it away and you diminish the game. How else will they settle differences on the ice?

Iain McKay
St Andrews, Scotland
Toronto Maple Leafs

I think fighting has a place in the game. It can change momentum big time or it can be used to send a message. I hate how some players take cheap shots at stars and because fighting has become a little less common they don't necessarily have to take responsibility for their actions. Headshots would be a lot less common if the players responsible had to stand up to a tough fighter on their next shift. Saying that though, I'd hate to see another Todd Bertuzzi!

James Bird
Burnley, England
Pittsburgh Penguins

Well, I guess like most fans I love it at the right times. It certainly pumps up the crowd in the building! (Staubitz-Tootoo, oh yeah!). I'm sure I'm not the only one who enjoys seeing the likes of Sidney Crosby getting involved or receiving a fist sandwich.
Not too keen on the 'Goons' overshadowing quality hockey though, but fighting still has its place as a unique aspect of our sport.

Jason Dunn
Woking, England
San Jose Sharks

I can't see hockey without fighting. Hockey is a contact sport, fighting has always been seen as a way to energise your team, protect your star and goalie and I have no problem with two guys agreeing to go. I do have a problem with targeting a player, taking him out to give your team a better chance, or hitting guys into the boards head first. Now I'm not a ref so I don't know how they deal with fighting - how they tell what penalties are to be called - so I don't have a solution, just an observation.

Jonathan Northall

My other concern is that the equipment players now use is so hard, the players themselves are bigger and quicker and the game itself is so much faster that any hit could result in injury - but again, an observation I have no answers.

Joan Chisholm
Washington, England
Edmonton Oilers

I like fighting in hockey, providing that both combatants are happy to fight, and there are no cheap shots. I believe there was, formerly, a place in the league for much rougher, more 'imposed fights', but, in the 'new' NHL I don't see a reason for the overly violent, and vicious, fighting of old.

Joe Alderson
Stoke-on-Trent, England
Detroit Red Wings

I think it is needed to protect your team. I support the Bruins, and as such, Thornton is our "enforcer", although we have plenty of other guys that will drop the gloves. And if you look, teams are less likely to take cheap shots against the Bruins, as they will dish out their own form of punishment.

Kimmi Noble
Sheffield, England
Boston Bruins

I love the fighting in the NHL. I love that a player is able to spark his team or the crowd by fighting an opponent. I want the fights to be fair though. No surprise jumping on another player. Get the gloves off, helmets too, and then let them fight! The fights are an important part of the games, but I don't want the games to get spoiled by fighting. In those cases, the refs need to do their job really well to get the game going.

Kristina Stryhn Laursen
Copenhagen, Denmark
Toronto Maple Leafs / New York Islanders

No matter what we do, physicality and fighting will always be a part of our sport. It's a tough game, an emotional game and one where the perfect release can be a good old scrap! It revs up your team mates, it can intimidate the other team and fans just love it! Whilst I would never use fighting as the 'be all and end all' in enticing friends along, when ever I do speak to them or they come along, they always ask, "will there be fights?" More often than not there won't be a fight, but they enjoy it anyway. A fast paced end to end game can be just as fun to watch than a fight filled one! Fighting does not define hockey, but it sure does have a place in hockey!

Mark Woodcock
Macclesfield, England
Phoenix Coyotes

I'm not against fighting, if a heated matchup boils over that can be huge fun to watch. I hate the staged stuff though, it just ruins a game. Thankfully it seems to be on the decline. Really though, fighting is a part of hockey and people tune in because of it so to be thoroughly against it is to be against an integral part of the sport.

Matt Merritt
Portsmouth, England
Toronto Maple Leafs

What I love about hockey is the physical part. For me, there is nothing like a great open-ice hit. Or even better, an offensive hit with the puck under control. When it comes to fighting I can definitely make it without it. I think that the worst part of the NHL is the fighting. Two guys who drop their gloves and then tries to make the best out of the fight. I say there is nothing more meaningless in any sport. Standing up for your goalie who has been run over by an opponent is a different thing. That is a natural part of hockey. Hockey must be a sport that allows big hits and pushing and shoving in front of the goal. Unprovoked violence as we have seen (Shea Weber taking Henrik Zetterberg's head and smash it into the glass over and over again, for example) has to be stopped. Not only for the player's safety but for the signals it sends to the young kids watching the game. I also get afraid when two tired players stand, holding each other, with their helmets rolling around on the ice and one of them losing their balance and smashes to the ice. It's just a matter of time before someone gets seriously injured.

Mattias Boström
Stockholm, Sweden
Colorado Avalanche

Fighting has a place in the NHL, when used correctly it brings a whole arena to its feet and can resurge a team on the ice. I also feel it brings new fans to the game, people start watching hockey to see a fight then fall in love with the rest of the game. The NHL just has to make sure these players are protected, and given the necessary support on and off the ice.

Nathan Cartmel
Bristol, England (now Tampa, FL, USA)
Tampa Bay Lightning

Fighting is alright as part of the sport just it should never be the main part of the sport, in my opinion, team toughness is much better hard checking etc.

Phil Holding
Nottingham, England
Washington Capitals

I'm all for fighting in the NHL. Yes it has it's good points and bad points, but at the end of the day it's all part of the entertainment package that makes ice hockey such a great sport to watch. The anti-fighting crowd will point to the 3 deaths of Derek Boogaard, Wade Belak and Rick Rypien, all of who were enforcers during their playing careers. The league does need to look into the possible link of head injuries. I like fighting and you should look no further than the Philadelphia/Ottawa melee in 2004 or the brawls between Detroit and Colorado during their rivalry to appreciate fighting. Staged fights can be a little annoying at times as they often come across as fighting for fighting sake. More often than not though fights break out due to necessity, partly, because referees have lost some control over the game. The crowd reaction after a fight is almost as loud as when a goal is scored. Fights can change the momentum of games. Fights may not be perfect but they are an integral part of the game.

Ray Skeates
Basingstoke, England
Philadelphia Flyers

I think that fighting still has a place in hockey. My reasons are that the game needs to still be able to police itself as some players in the league today are dirty enough but take away the fighting and they will get even dirtier and a lot more injuries would incur as a result. Another reason is to give a team a spark and get the energy going when they are losing a game and can't get into it but the biggest reason is the fans. Most fans like to see a fight and it either takes the crowd out of the game or gets them into it, if the building is quiet.

Ice Hockey Nights in Europe

No player is forced to drop the gloves and fight so as long as it's a personal choice for a player whether or not to fight then I can't see the harm in it.

Raymond Jackson
Ballymena, Northern Ireland
Calgary Flames

I don't have a problem with the fighting its part and partial of the game and all hockey fans know this and understand this always been in every era. Get rid of it and you lose a piece of the game that completes the puzzle. I think it has improved a couple of years they brought in a rule which has reduced the number of fights. As a fan I don't think it incites anything its just two people letting out their emotions in a very completive environment

Rebecca Hindle
Manchester, England
Florida Panthers

I like it but only if both players agree to do so. If you want to go at it with someone then it has to be returned. I'd also like to see a maximum number of fights allowed in a game (say 3), and if it goes over that then teams get fined for not controlling their players, as it gets ridiculous when there are fights galore.

Richard Trowbridge
Cheltenham, England
Toronto Maple Leafs

Recent media coverage has portrayed fighting in hockey as a throwback to frontier times with scraps occurring on the ice, and on the benches, for no better reason than I didn't like the way he looked at me. Whilst it may seem that the reasons for some of the fights are petty, they are usually the build up of events from previous games between the teams or history between the players involved. I believe there is a place for fighting in the sport but the penalties for doing so should be greater. There is a need to protect your high profile players from excessive checks, persistent fouls, boarding and slashing but the players should know that dropping the gloves will lead to greater time in the box or in the changing rooms.

Jonathan Northall

There will then need to be a judgement call as to whether the sacrifice is warranted to defend your players and your team.

Rob Aherne
Stafford, England
Pittsburgh Penguins

I've got to be honest here and say that it was fighting that got me hooked on hockey in the first place. The excitement, brutality and sheer bizarreness of watching some of the early season scraps between Sheffield Steelers and Nottingham Panthers, particularly ex-NHL'ers Dennis Vial and Barry Nieckar, got me coming back for more as the 2000-01 ISL season progressed. However I soon learned and understood the place that fighting actually had in the game and the context in which it should, in my opinion, be, I began to appreciate the finer points of hockey. I believe that fighting still has an important role to play in the sport but the day of the traditional enforcer or goon has well and truly gone. I believe that fighting can help to police things that are perhaps missed by the officials or say settle a 'score' in a more honourable way. I hate to see two goons face off - completely out of context - just because it's what they have to do. No, I'd much rather see a fight like the one between Max Talbot and Dan Carcillo that sparked the Penguins dramatic comeback in game 6 of the 2009 Play-off 1st round series against the Flyers. It was a fight with purpose and in context. Hopefully, the tragic deaths of Wade Belak and Rick Rypien will ultimately end the traditional role of the enforcer, who has to earn his living by having his head pummelled in and by pummelling his opponent's head night after night.

Rob Howe
Sheffield, England
Pittsburgh Penguins

Growing up in Pennsylvania in the 1970's meant one thing for hockey fans: guaranteed fights with blood whenever Philly's "Broad Street Bullies" met up with my Pittsburgh Penguins....and it was so much fun to watch! While I am against blatant hits to the head or knees that are done specifically to injure star players, I am a big fan of "Old Time Hockey" and the fights that go along with it! All fans instantly love their teams' "enforcer" and the scrappy fourth line guy who you just know is going to drop the gloves the first chance he gets. Hockey fights have been part of the game for over 100 years now and is unique to this sport. In any other team competition having a fist fight during a game means an immediate ejection and probable suspension, whereas in hockey it usually just results in a 5 or 10 minute penalty! Nothing gets the home crowd pumped up more than a fight, and it's even better when it's a bench clearing brawl!

Robert Campbell
Pittsburgh, USA (now Uppsala, Sweden)
Pittsburgh Penguins

Personally I enjoy hockey fights, it adds to the intensity of the game and can really get a crowd going, seeing a tough guy from one team drop gloves with an opponent from the other gets me as a fan excited. At the end of the day the players that fight are big guys that can take punches so I don't see any problem with it.

Robert Weaver
Gloucestershire, England
Ottawa Senators

Who doesn't like a good fight? It just shows how passionate the guys are about the game. Either if it's to revenge a teammate or just from a sheer hate towards the opponent. As long as it is a fair fight both guys want to get into, I have nothing against it.

Štěpánka Černá
Dolní Němčí, Czech Republic
Winnipeg Jets

Fighting is an essential part of hockey. Hockey players skate around with razor sharp blades on their feet and composite carbon fibre sticks in their hands. If they are not allowed to settle their grievances with their fists, they will settle it using other means – and perhaps the weapons they are carrying around with them. Stick penalties are certainly more prevalent in continental Europe where fighting is strongly discouraged and even legislated against by extreme penalties. Of course, we must be mindful of concussions and player safety and I think this is combated by applying more severe penalties (fines, suspensions etc.) for fights that occur after legal hits. Fighting in response to an illegal action is ok – but not simply because "our star player got hit and we can't have that". The suitable response in that case is to lay a big hit on their star player.

Stuart Coles
Coventry, England
LA Kings

Jonathan Northall

The issue with fighting in hockey is that people in the stands are either one way or the other. Nobody is sat there thinking 'I don't mind'. They're either upset about it, or overjoyed. Having read much on the subject, it's clear that I am on the side that is for fighting. The game never had the massive cheap shots, the huge concussions and the serious boarding, until the instigator rule was implemented. If opposing players were scoring and playing well, you'd either try to provoke them, or you'd try to scare them. Either way, the opposition enforcer would usually then start a shift and then you'd have willing combatants ready to go. I think the fact that the majority of fights are within 'the code' shows that there is not a lot of thugs simply 'gooning' around punching anyone who comes nearby, but that both players know the rules and what is expected of them. The fact is that fighting is an almost sure-fire way of firing up your team, and the fans. Until that stops working, then the fighting will stay.

Stuart Wilson
York, England
Detroit Red Wings

I love fighting. I can't wait until I see a goalie fight live. I've only seen them on YouTube, but they look awesome. I can understand the new found concern with fighting, but you only have to be in the arena when a fight breaks out to realise how popular they are. You don't hear the crowd boo at the prospect of a fight. Ideally you want to see two matched opponents as on occasion the mismatches can be brutal to watch, but both combatants were up for it at the get go, so you appreciate the 'chops' of the underdog. A good fight can change momentum in games, my Flyers' fan fiancé will hate me for mentioning Carcillo versus Talbot, but this is a prime example of it. Even he knew it was a bad fight to engage in and the result changed, in part because of it. If fighting was banned, players would find other ways to take out their frustration and this could lead to worse injuries to unsuspecting players. The best players could be targeted, and I doubt the league would want that.

Vicki Morgan
Basingstoke, England
Minnesota Wild

Personally I am against fighting. I feel that Hockey is Hockey and if people want to watch fighting they should go and watch boxing or wrestling. I know over here in the UK many parents against their kids playing hockey because of fighting and I feel that perhaps over here in the UK anyway, hockey would become a bigger sport if fighting was stopped! So I am against fighting!

James Cartwright
Cardiff, Wales
New York Islanders

Yes, every time you see a hockey fight, it's an incredible spectacle and the crowd in the stands love their own heroes which stand up for their respective captains or stars. Honestly, it doesn't need fights for a good hockey game. And everyone read the stories about the enormous pressure under which the so called enforcers live. The suicides from 2011 have shown that. That's why in my opinion the league should try to reduce fights by immediate game misconduct penalties instead of the large number of roughing calls. I think that will prevent some guys from fighting.

Alexander, Daniela & Marek Neumann
Schwäbisch Hall, Germany
Tampa Bay Lightning

This debate will rumble on and on and on, more than likely even beyond our own lifetimes. Personally, I believe fighting is part of what makes hockey what it is and is the residue of a game that is played physically and at an extremely rapid pace. When you play at such a high skill level and put up with some of the roughest punishment dished out in any professional sport, emotions will tip, blood will boil and the gloves, alas, will always come off. There are players whose stock-in-trade is specifically fighting and this is what I don't agree with. There are some big guys in the NHL. I recall a fight between Chris Pronger (then of the St Louis Blues) and Derian Hatcher (then of the Dallas Stars). Both stood over 6ft 3, both were absolute mammoths and neither did themselves any harm in squaring off in a completely random and spontaneous fight. The fact that fighting is penalized in the league and mass (or line) brawls continue to draw fines against the responsible club(s) but if someone who you don't see coming, hits you into the boards, dropping you on your backside, you should absolutely take the fight back to them. Keep it spontaneous and do away with the 'purpose-built' player and you keep something which many fans see as one of the purest aspects of the sport. After all, if you take away that spontaneity, you leave a lot of players with no fire in their belly and each guy who suits up - whether it's in the NHL or otherwise - knows fighting and standing up for yourself is all part of the game.
As long as it isn't racially motivated, it isn't taken too far and players understand they all have a duty of care to each other then I have no issue

Jonathan Northall

with it.

Chris Bluff
Stockton-On-Tees, England
Dallas Stars

Fighting in hockey is kind of a guilty pleasure for me. It's fun and exciting to watch and I wouldn't want it to go away. If I look at it objectively, there isn't really a reason to have fighting in the game anymore, other then it being entertaining. The argument that it keeps the game clean is overrated in my opinion, the fights where someone defends a teammate after an illegal check or his goalie after he got bumped are the best ones, but they only make for a small percentage of all fights. During the most important time of the year, the playoffs, you rarely see any fights at all. The players that are only there to fight are sitting in the press-box and those who can fight and play usually don't fight either, because at the end of the day the risk of getting injured or getting an extra-penalty is higher then the perceived advantage you have from "getting the crowd" going. Looking at the grand scheme of the fighting debate, I'd probably say I'm neutral. I don't see fighting as the heart of the game that has to be defended at all costs, like some old schoolers seem to, but I also don't want it to be banned. I'd say in the end, the risks and gains from fighting are pretty-balanced and the game will be as fine with it as it would be without.

David Trippler
Mainz, Germany
Buffalo Sabres

For me fighting needs to be strategic and spontaneous if it wants to stay a part of the ever changing face of hockey. I know a lot of people who are against the notion of dropping the gloves, and see it as 'unsportsmanlike' but exactly what kind of fighting are they talking about? Just because I take a fight-friendly stance doesn't mean I enjoy watching staged bouts, or mismatched pairings where one guy is picking another, weaker guy for the sake of his own ego. The kind of fighting I love to watch is when the fight is a pivot to change the momentum of the game first and foremost. That to me is tactical, certainly there will always be a degree of 'heat of the moment' to it, which is important because it rules out the staged element, but it's not just brutality for brutality's sake either. Fighting is often about players standing up for one another when the chips are down, delivering a vital morale boost that's more about pride and about momentum, than about wanting to cause serious injury and lasting damage. That's the kind of fighting I like to see stay in the game. Though I'm not going to deny, the odd purely personal on-ice vendetta can really add spice right at the start to an otherwise lack lustre match-up! Whether we like fights or not, I think hockey fans have to except that the role of the career 'goon' is being eradicated from the game. Guys on the fourth line are now expected to play their share of minutes and that must be a good thing. No one likes to see veterans suffering with mental and physical health problems after years of abuse. All in all, more skill and fewer casualties can only be better for the game. That's why I think fighting is naturally evolving with the game to become safer and that's why I think it should stay. Who said hockey was for the faint hearted anyway?

Eilis Phillips
Belfast, Northern Ireland
Boston Bruins

I hate the put-up jobs that are the pre-planned fights. A fight that results from temper "how dare you do that" kind of thing I can understand and kind of approve. Having said that, I hate the fights that result from a legal hit and players want to bully that.

Elliott Hall
Sheffield, England
Toronto Maple Leafs

I think hockey and fighting are strictly connected; there can't be hockey without fighting. As hockey is a sport also fighting should be sport related. If it happens, for example, when a player stands up for a team mate hit hard by an opponent, it's part of the game and can also be fun to watch. Sometimes it seems that payers fighting each other are dancing on the ice. When fighting is not spontaneous, when is planned before its happening, when players fight just to fight (even if only because they think they have to fight to entertain the audience), well in my humble opinion it's not real hockey fighting, and it's not fun to watch. So, where I stand on the fighting debate? Maybe in the middle: I hope fighting will be part of the game forever, but players should respect the rules of hockey fighting; if they're not able to, it could be useful to mark fighting bound even if running the risk to slowly eliminate it from the game.

Emanuela Pozzi
Cernusco sul Naviglio, Italy
New Jersey Devils

Personally I enjoy fighting in hockey as long as it's not staged. If it's a reaction to a bad hit on one of your team's star players or rookies, for example, I think it's a good way to show that those type things are not acceptable. But when it's just two goons using it as a way to entertain the crowd I'd rather they stuck to boxing or UFC. I also don't like the instigator rule for fighting as I think a bad hit is the instigation rather than the player looking to defend team mates!

Hana Imiolczyk
Merthyr Tydfil, Wales
Washington Capitals

I'm for fighting in the sense of it being a part and parcel of the sport, but against it when it overtakes the sport. For example, there was a New Jersey Devils and New York Rangers game in which the head coaches just sent out lines to fight at the start of the game and came, with the drop of the puck, the drop of the gloves. It was what the game was largely remembered for and that's not right for any sport (well, except boxing, martial arts, etc.) It's tough for the NHL though, because if they try too many limits on what fighting cannot include, it almost suggests that they're also condoning some parts of it. At the moment it's more like they tolerate it. If they start saying what can't be done, then it will be allowing the things that "can be done", instead of just tolerating them.

James Willis
Watford, England
New York Rangers

My stance on the fighting debate is maybe a bit difficult to explain. Hockey is such a physical game that inevitably there will be times when tempers boil over. As a player, I have no problem with fights in a game if they have some context behind them, i.e. some one has taken a late run at one of your team mates or goalie. However, I don't think that the stereotypical enforcer has any space in modern hockey. The game has become faster and more entertaining to watch. I actually remember when I was watching Boston Bruins versus Washington Capitals in Boston at the start of the 2010-2011 season. Within the first second of the game there was a fight between Shawn Thornton and a Washington player whose NHL career probably was just that one game. The crowd went nuts, but I didn't get excited by it as you could see it happening from the two agreeing to do it off the opening faceoff. To me, that style of fighting is a dying breed in the NHL. Yes, the fights are fun to watch, but only when there's something behind it, not two enforcers just deciding that the game needs a bit of spice and doing it off a faceoff after agreeing it formally. There's a code in hockey which is often used to settle some disputes that result from outside of the play. The code has been there for years and I don't personally see that moving away any time soon. When it comes to your prototypical goons (as portrayed in the movie "Goon"), I fear it is a dying breed.

Janne Virtanen
Hameenlinna, Finland (now Basingstoke, Eng)
Montreal Canadiens

I have no issue with the fighting its part and parcel with Hockey, I don't like the stage fighting i.e Devils-Rangers game where both team reacted to each other's line ups and fought before the puck even dropped, with the concussion issue in the NHL and the link it has to fighting it has to be more controlled.

Junaid Hussain
Nottingham, England
Detroit Red Wings

I would say I'm standing somewhere in the middle. I can understand both points of view on fighting. I'm neither completely against it nor am I a huge supporter. For me, fighting is a part of hockey and should probably stay in the game. I think it's better if players go at it one on one when things get heated rather than having someone cheap shot someone from behind. What I don't like though are "stage fights". These don't make much sense to me.

Katerina Brzonova
Zlin, Czech Republic
Tampa Bay Lightning

In an ideal world, there would be no need for fighting in a sport. Referees would pick and up on and effectively punish every rule infraction committed by a player in the course of a game, and it would satisfy all involved. However in a sport as fast and hard-hitting as ice hockey, it's nigh on impossible to reach this violence-free utopian idyll and if we're honest with ourselves, as fans, would we really want it to? One of the finest things to witness in hockey is a well-timed and clean hit. It's like tackling in football; however, instead of being a dying art, over-punished and increasingly disappearing from a player's arsenal as they fear the consequences of health and safety paranoid, card-happy referees, it's still a prized skill in ice hockey. Or at least, it should be. However it's widely acknowledged that the game is speeding up, and with this increase in speed comes an increased risk of injury. It's far from a perfect system, as it is up to referees to make decisions based on what they see in front of them, which sometimes, may look worse than it is. Or they may not see at all. And even when they make a decision that looks to be correct, team-mates of the victim of a particularly hard hit may still take exception. The waters are undoubtedly muddy. Self-policing in ice hockey has been part of the game since its inception and I for one think there's something quite noble about allowing space in a rulebook for players to air their grievances in the relative safety of the arena, rather than allowing them to fester and perhaps take on nastier connotations as the season progresses. There's no getting around the fact that ice hockey is lightning fast and hard as nails and those playing have to be prepared to accept the consequences. I think there is a place for fighting in hockey as long as it is reactionary and not pre-meditated. The frisson of tensions and emotions boiling over makes for an atmosphere unlike that of any other sport and it would be a shame to lose that from the game. Honest and spontaneous enforcement is a very different animal than festering resentments leading to one player setting out to intentionally hurt another player. The latter should never be allowed. The former, along with a more robust and consistent system of checks and balances across the league, should prevent it from ever happening.

Katy Parles
Newcastle upon Tyne, England
Calgary Flames

Fighting is one of the most contentious issues in the NHL and divides everyone from fans to officials. I dislike the "arranged" fighting where two guys decide on the ice they are just going to fight. That to me is meaningless and has nothing to do with the game. However if a player goes in to defend a team mate after a dirty hit or play by the opposition and that ends up in a fight then fine. Hockey is and has always been a passionate sport, no matter at which level it is played. If you totally eradicate fighting then I believe less talented players will target the stars of the game knowing there will be no recourse for their actions during the game. With the NHL not keen on suspending players for their actions either, I think banning fighting would be to the detriment of NHL hockey.

Mark Rackham
Kent, England
Toronto Maple Leafs

Ice Hockey Nights in Europe

I'm on the fence. It's very entertaining when not staged (agreed before the game). It shows real emotions and shares real emotions. People like to see intensity and how much players care. A spirited, non-staged fight is huge. On the other hand we know about concussions and other injuries. I'd rather see players remove helmets and gloves - as in "let's settle this here and now, come on!" but they also have to stop throwing rivals on the ice, MMA style, to look better in the eyes of the crowd. Landing on ice and probably hitting your head is when injuries usually happen. Is this doable?

Michał Pręgowski
Warsaw, Poland
Vancouver Canucks

Hockey is a physical game, and I like that you can stick up for your teammates when an opponent oversteps the mark with a dirty hit. If your opponents are going to have an agitator, then you have to be given a way of combating it, if you take fighting away you may see the dirtiest guys in the league get even worse. When it starts to get gratuitous it doesn't look good, for example when all 10 guys go at it from the opening face-off it's just pointless no matter how much animosity there is between rivals or whoever. You can't take it out of the game though when almost all the players say they want it to stay.

Mike Fuller
Newcastle, England
Colorado Avalanche

I don't think fighting will ever be removed from the game and, to a point, I support that. However, given it's an emotional game, it's only fair the fights are a product of that and not a staged circus attraction between two "players" who's only job is to "play" two minutes a night. It should be organic. Maybe the best example would be the famous Iginla versus Lecavalier bout - that is organic, that I support.

Mislav Jantoljak
Zagreb, Croatia
Pittsburgh Penguins / Toronto Maple Leafs

I am indifferent. In European hockey we rarely have fights and relatively few powerplays whencompared to the NHL, but I understand that across the pond it is seen as part of the sport. As longas it doesn't get out of control or excessively brutal then I don't have a problem with it, especially if those involved are punished suitably. Many fans enjoy fighting and it would perhaps turn them off it was removed.

Steve McCaskill
Maidstone, England
Columbus Blue Jackets

I find fighting in hockey entertaining sometimes, but I don't like it when it gets nasty. By all means have a fight, try to turn the momentum, send a message to the other team or whatnot. But don't try to injure on purpose. Also, don't take part in mismatched fights - pick on someone your own size!

Tim Barnes
Cambridge, England (born in New Jersey, USA)
Philadelphia Flyers

In my opinion fighting in hockey is all part of the game as long as it's for the right reasons. I'm all for fighting when it comes to sticking up for your team mates, but am not in favour of the enforcer mentality, where guys are just on the ice to fight. I think those players are slowly dying out of the game anyway, the game is too quick for those types of players to compete anymore.

Tom Harding
Isle of Wight, England
Pittsburgh Penguins

In the fighting debate, I would say I do not think it should ever be banned as such. The nature of the speed and physical contact in the sport make it very much unique from many other sports. Most fans seem to enjoy fights although personally I do not agree with 'staged fights' where players have pretty much agreed to fight each other before a game has even started. If, during the heat of battle, two players are both willing combatants then I believe this should be allowed to happen, as long as officials do a good job in stepping in during a very one sided fight or if a player looks seriously hurt etc. I would, however, prefer fights to happen between players in a team for their skills rather than players who in reality only ever go on the ice to intimidate and fight.

Tony Harrison
Rutland, England
Toronto Maple Leafs

8 WHAT ARE YOUR HOPES FOR THE FUTURE OF YOUR TEAM?

Stanley Cup. Let's get that answer out there straight away. It is an obvious answer for all teams. It is the ultimate prize and every fan wants it for their team. Whether your team is a past winner or striving for the first, all fans have a burning desire to see Lord Stanley take residence in for twelve months.

Fans have more modest aims too. Be it reclaiming former glory or establishing themselves as playoff contenders, the passion of fans emanates from their submissions. Interestingly, the timing of asking the questions was such that the Maple Leafs were still on an illusive quest to make the playoffs again. Each Leafs fan who sent in a submission was only too eager to lament on this malady that had befell the franchise. However, the 2012-13 season would see playoff hockey return to Toronto and render pages of the book useless. I am glad for them that this is the case. In particular I'm pleased for Mark Rackham, who has been a great supporter of this project, who embodies all the qualities of a European hockey fan that most should aspire to emulate.

The NHL and NHLPA have created a sprawling juggernaut of a league, where it is easy to be competitive, but very hard to lift Lord Stanley's cup. It's a league where 10 points separates the 'success' of home-ice in the playoffs and the ignominy of a lottery pick, with very few teams having the pieces to 'go all the way.' My hopes for the future for the Ducks have to be tempered; we bought our cup in 2007, and many teams are currently queuing up with their cheque-books before our turn comes again.
My hopes are that the Ducks retain the soul of the franchise when Teem retires, and that the love of the game he exemplifies is continued, and that we remain a playoff team more often than not – meaning the gross waste of talent we saw in 11/12 doesn't happen again.
I want Smith-Pelly, Fowler and Etem grow into elite-potential players, and Hiller to establish himself in everyone's list of the top 5 NHL goaltenders. Also, remaining the only team in California to win the Stanley Cup would be nice as would getting a win against Nashville before I leave this life!

Allan Allison
Bristol, England
Anaheim Ducks

To win another Stanley Cup and to work on the power play more because it's always rubbish come playoff time.

Amy Hill
Camberley, England
Boston Bruins

To win the cup. There really isn't more to say or to wish for. The last few seasons have been pretty disappointing for us and I think in my (short) time as a Sabres-fan, I haven't even see us win a single playoff-series, so seeing a series-win in the playoffs would be a nice start. But in the end it's all about winning the cup and that has to be the ultimate hope/goal for the future.

David Trippler
Mainz, Germany
Buffalo Sabres

My hopes for the Hawks are high; we have a high-energy young core that needs to remain together. Another Stanley Cup in Chicago would light the touch paper in my opinion. I believe the current crop of draftees (last 3 years) is strong enough to take this team to another level.

Nathan Hollis
Norwich, England
Chicago Blackhawks

I have been the Colorado Avalanche fan since my 10 years old. I have never lost the hope for the Stanley Cup. Never ever. And I will never do. New season means the old dream – get another cup, win 16 games in the off-season. Never give up and play for their fans. European fans. Worldwide fans. For every fan in the world. It´s all about commitment– you can notice these words in the locker room. Only die-hard fans could understand it. The passion, the effort and the commitment: because of that, Colorado Avalanche will win Stanley Cup in the next season. It´s all about commitment. You know?

David Púchovský
Bratislava, Slovakia
Colorado Avalanche

For the Avs, keep building on their decent season with excellent young players and build a team around them. Maybe they won't hit the heights of where they were, but they are improving. As for Boston, they have to be looking at a new starting goalie. Rask is impressive but he is no Thomas.

Andy Parsons
London, England
Colorado Avalanche

I'd really like the Avs to make the post-season, even if the Avs were to be swept. The kids need to gain as much experience as possible. Being exposed to the play-offs would also make them stronger mentally in the regular season. Another thing I hope for is that the Avs sign the guys that need to be. Matt Duchene and Ryan O'Reilly being the priorities, but the signings of guys like Steve Downy and Jamie McMinn are as important. Just don't break up the core you spent so much time building. This team is full of character. Another thing I really wish for is getting a full-time goalie coach. If the Avs are clever and want to end the endless goalie troubles they had for the last couple of seasons, they need to bring in a full-time coach. All in all, I'm not hoping for a Stanley Cup in 5 seasons, I'm good with the Avs becoming a contender, not just a bubble team playing for their play-off chance at the seasons end. The future is bright in Denver, we'll just have to wait and see what it brings.

Michal Hežely
Michalovce, Slovakia
Colorado Avalanche

Obviously I'd want the Avs to win the Stanley Cup at some point, but everyone is going to say that. I'd be satisfied with making the playoffs more often than not, with the occasional deep run to get excited about. I think the future is bright with players like Landeskog, O'Reilly, Duchene, Johnson and Varlamov along with some of the prospects that will hopefully develop in to NHL calibre. In the short term, I can see Colorado being a bubble team for a couple of seasons, unless the owners decide to splash the cash in free agency to add a desperately needed high scoring winger and/or elite defenseman. There's certainly the cap space available to do that, but if the roster building is going as planned then I don't mind being patient.

Mike Fuller
Newcastle, England
Colorado Avalanche

There is just one thing that counts. The Stanley Cup! What the organization needs to do is to get their hands on a couple of established players in order to reach the standard of the good old days. First: A solid defensive defender, like Adam Foote once was. The team has to have a solid ground to lay against. Second: A defender with great offensive skills, like Erik Karlsson of the Senators. Who can make a great impact on the power play? Third: Every team needs a star or two. Tampa has Stamkos and Los Angeles has Dustin Brown. Philadelphia has Giroux and Washington has Ovechkin. Enough said! The Avs hasn't got any of these three profiles today. Perhaps some of today's players might get there in a couple of years but in order to become a constant top-of-standings team with the opportunity to fight for the Cup every year this is what I think has to be done. The Avs need a mix of young and hungry players like Gabriel Landeskog with older, experienced players.

Mattias Boström
Stockholm, Sweden
Colorado Avalanche

I have two hopes, firstly that the team stays in Columbus and secondly, we have a competitive team capable of at least reaching the play-offs, Financial problems, the issue of stadium ownership and dreadful on-ice performances mean that I genuinely fear for the future of the team in Columbus. In a city where the only professional rivals are Columbus Crew in the MLS, it should be possible to establish a niche and a hockey legacy, even if the presence of Ohio State University ensures that college football dominates the sporting agenda. We may never get another chance to create a competitive team again, not in Columbus anyway, and without a decent team, fans will begin to start voting with their feet and stop attending games. It's been 13 years since the Blue Jackets were founded and just one play-off appearance seems like an insufficient return.

Steve McCaskill
Maidstone, England
Columbus Blue Jackets

With no playoff hockey in Dallas for 5 straight seasons, my hope is to make it to the post-season next time around. Despite the team not being able to get it done where it counted last season, I think the future is pretty bright and I am very optimistic ahead of next season. My biggest hope is that we can make a couple of big additions in the off-season. Canadian businessman Tom Galrdi became the new owner of the Stars in the middle of the

Ice Hockey Nights in Europe

2011/12 season, and this guy seems the real deal. He has said to GM Niuwendyk that the funds are there if he wants to make a recruit or 2. The thing Galardi did first was boost the attendance levels at the American Airlines Center, something that needed drastically changing. With a decent core group of players, a couple of big recruits and a good crowd in to watch some hockey, I am really looking forward to next season.

George Royle
Malmesbury, England
Dallas Stars

As a Redwings fan I'm hoping for continued success in the Central division but with the likes of the Predators, Blues, Blackhawks always being competitive and losing the central division title for the first time in many years It was a tough pill to swallow. Hopefully we are able to get younger as team with the likes of Holmstrom and Lindstrom at the end of their careers with a new core group able to reclaim the central title as well as winning the Stanley Cup at least a couple of times over the next 10 years but with the league being so competitive as well as balanced it will be a tough road ahead.

Junaid Hussain
Nottingham, England
Detroit Red Wings

The Red Wings have had over 20 years of success, the biggest ambition I have for my team if for us to just continue to be a contending team, consistently, year to year, for a long time to come. Another cup final, and maybe biggest a 12th Stanley cup would also be amazing, perhaps the ambition I have for my team, but my most realistic, and desired ambition, if for the Red Wings to be able to carry on playing, competitively, with guys like Nicklas Lidstrom, Pavel Datsyuk, Henrik Zetterberg, Niklas Kronwall all at high levels, for years to come, as they are a group of players that I love to see on ice. I guess there is no real, huge, drastic change I desire in the Wing's future, it's as simple as these four words: more of the same!

Joe Alderson
Stoke-on-Trent, England
Detroit Red Wings

My hopes for my team are simply in two parts. I hope that the Red Wings will continue to draft wisely, and nurture their young players through the processes of the AHL. Their introduction to the NHL is gradual, which seems to work well, as players such as Datsyuk, Zetterberg, Kronwall, Ericsson, Holmstrom, Franzen, Helm, and Jimmy Howard all came from smart drafting. Zetterberg and Datsyuk were late drafts and look at the effect they've made in Detroit. This kind of young player production is what keeps Detroit in the Playoffs season after season. Every now and then a trade will be required (such as with Ian White), but it's usual that a younger player steps up and into the gap left by an outgoing player. Nyquist, Kindl, Emmerton, Smith and Tatar are the future, and I hope they get their chance to shine. I hope that my team will start a 15-season domination of league and playoffs, posting record breaking points and goals. Not too much to ask is it?

Stuart Wilson
York, England
Detroit Red Wings

I would love the Oilers to keep a core of players over the next few years so they can build their future to include a Stanley Cup! Or at least make it to the playoffs. I would like a return to the days when the Oilers were a top team not welcome in any other barns, booed by the opposition fans (always a sign you are doing something right for your team!), with new fans jumping on the bandwagon and old fans finally getting something to cheer about after years of putting on a brave face whilst watching Calgary drop out of the running for a playoff place and Vancouver getting beaten in their cup run

Joan Chisholm
Washington, England
Edmonton Oilers

To make more playoffs and not wait 12 years to make the next one and to win more trophies the SE Division title and win Conference Trophy to make the Stanley Cup Finals and go one better than in 1996 and win the Stanley Cup. Bring the trophy to the Sunshine State, South Florida, and prove the doubters wrong that Ice Hockey can prosper in Miami with the dedicated fans. Have a Winter Classic in Florida versus Tampa Bay! I don't see a reason why not it would be a great feet and a brilliant match no love lost and tensions would be high this would also show that NHL cared about teams in Florida.

Rebecca Hindle
Manchester, England
Florida Panthers

Ice Hockey Nights in Europe

Right now, I'm hoping for another Stanley Cup win in the next 3-4 seasons. The Kings have gone through a rebuilding phase and have come out the other side stronger and better. After that, I'm hoping for a sustained period of competitiveness; challenging at the top of the NHL standings for years to come. The Kings have been a boom and bust team for a long time, without ever capturing the cup. Because of this, it has been very difficult to attract the top players here. That trend has started to break. Mike Richards came in Summer 2011 and hopefully his success will attract other top free agents here. Not too many mind, as I'd like to be developing stars from within as well like Jonathan Quick, Dustin Brown and Anze Kopitar, who really are the core of the current side. I don't think I want too much...

Stuart Coles
Coventry, England
LA Kings

For the Wild, it will probably be baby steps. Finish with winning record. Qualify for playoffs. Gain experience. Win Cup. Of course, this could be fast-tracked in free agency. I didn't like the Gilbert/Schultz trade at first, but I've since learned he is good friends with Parise, who is friends with Suter. Landing both was a dream, but gave Vancouver some competition for the division. We have a lot of good young players; most reached the Calder Cup final with the Aeros. Mike Yeo coached that team to. Familiarity with the players is a great advantage. We do need more scoring, we also need less injuries to key players, we can't continue to be this unlucky with them. Another top 10 pick in the draft, we need prospects on D, the draft is top heavy with defenseman. If we pick right, the future could be bright.

Vicki Morgan
Basingstoke, England
Minnesota Wild

As always, I will try to stay optimistic in my hopes for the future, I feel the Edmonton Oilers have a big opportunity in the future to build another dynasty, I can see success in their future for certain. Montreal should be able to find a way of turning things around, it will be a long tough journey but they will once again become great. The first thing they need to do though is work on their defence as they had leads but defence is what cost them.

Jonathan Northall

My main hope is for a Stanley Cup in Canada and I hope to see a Canadian team (except for Ottawa) winning the Cup.

Diarmuid Murray
Dublin, Rep of Ireland
Montreal Canadiens

With the Habs, there are many things that a fan wants. One thing that I wish that the team would do is to put together a team that doesn't look into whether a player or coach comes from a French-Canadian background. Habs being one of the perennial NHL franchises, there is a lot of politics involved around and in the team, which is something that I feel that affects the teams' play to a great extent and is something that I'd like to see less of. The Canadiens are facing a re-building phase but we have good crops of young players coming through.

Janne Virtanen
Hameenlinna, Finland (now Basingstoke, England)
Montreal Canadiens

Every hockey fan will tell you that he cares only about one thing - his team winning the Stanley Cup. I would lie if I told you that it's not the same in my case, because it is. Predators' winning the Cup is the biggest dream I have. But there are also many smaller (though still important) hopes for my team. First of all, I would mention sustaining the current identity of the Predators as a young, speedy, blue-collar, hard working, defence-oriented, well-coached and well-managed team. Secondly, signing pending free-agents to a long-term contracts. Another very important thing for me is sustaining the current trend of growth of the hockey market in Nashville area. Each year, more and more people come to the games. I got to know some of them, and they are wonderful people, deserving a good hockey team in their city. I'm very proud of what this team has gone through since the fire sale of 2007 (losing Peter Forsberg, Paul Kariya, Scott Hartnell, Kimmo Timonen, Tomas Vokoun, etc.) and since talks about possible relocation to Hamilton, up to establishing as a big force in the Western Conference last year. We all love such Cinderella stories. And they usually end well. Such an ending is my hope for the future of the Preds.

Paweł Jachowski
Siedlce, Poland
Nashville Predators

Ice Hockey Nights in Europe

That would be the hope and dream that most hockey fans around the world have for their team every year is another Stanley Cup! But in general I'm hoping we find a replacement for Marty, is that even possible well I honestly don't think there will ever be a goalie as good as Marty, but we need to find someone who is a top class goalie who can keep the puck out the net for us in seasons to come, as Hedburg is close to retirement also being only a little younger than Marty. Next is to get back are defensive force, in years past if The Devils took the lead you new we were keeping it or well you new it was highly likely! Now lately we have been getting leads and throwing the game away by letting in sloppy goals, a lot coming from silly mistakes and turnovers. Hopefully the addition of Adam Larsson to the roster will be a great defensive boost, he played a lot of games this season for a rookie player so hopefully in time he will turn into a superstar defender, especially with Scott Stevens coaching him.

Gavin Clarke
Bristol, England
New Jersey Devils

What do I want for my NY Rangers? Well...- The main and obvious thing I would like for them is to win the Stanley Cup within the next few years, be it next year or a little further down the line. Let's face it though; everyone wants that for his or her team, don't they? - In addition to this, I would like to see the Rangers continue with their process of drafting young players and developing them through the system instead of spending big bucks on the marquee free agents every time. - The more obscure thing I would like to see though is for the team to continue its work in the community, through organisations like the Garden of Dreams Foundation. After watching the HBO series and seeing what the players do in their off time, it made me proud to be a Rangers fan. I would also like to see the team continue to make gestures like ex-coach John Tortorella, who spoke regularly with young cerebral palsy sufferer Liam Traynor and makes gestures like giving him and his family tickets to the Winter Classic. Extremely kind thing to do and again, another reason to be proud of the Rangers organisation.

Daruish Gorgirzadeh
Bournemouth, England
New York Rangers

I'd obviously like to see a Stanley Cup win. Beyond that, there honestly isn't much I'd change in terms of the Rangers' future. The organisation is consistently integrating prospects into the line-up each season, drafting smartly under Gordie Clark's leadership, and has shown a clear desire not to sacrifice the future for a quick fix anymore.

Alex Nunn
Romford, England
New York Rangers

My hope for this team is that they win at least one Stanley Cup over the next few years. The nucleus of the team is there; it is littered with excellent young players: Stepan, Del Zotto, Hagelin, McDonagh. Combine this with the veteran leadership, Callahan, Giraidi and Staal are still the right side 30 and you have a potent combination of youth and experience. The Rangers won the Atlantic Division with 109 points this season, the highest since 2000-01. Furthermore, they finished in the top two of the division for the first time since 1993-94. My hope is days of squeaking into the play-offs on the last day and being reliant on other results are over. I would like them to add some more offense in the close season.

Ed Johnston
Somerset, England
New York Rangers

It sounds boring, but my hope for the future of the New York Rangers is simply more Stanley Cups. Many start up franchises will perhaps be hoping for team stability or to remain in a certain location, but with the New York Rangers they already have those things. They're a well-known, stable franchise that is hugely unlikely to ever move from the city of New York. Therefore my hopes are simply the same of those in the team itself, the ultimate prize in hockey, more Stanley Cups. Perhaps optimistically overtaking the Montreal Canadiens record for the most wins. Not that it could ever happen in my lifetime. Sadly.

James Willis
Watford, England
New York Rangers

I'm a Flyers fan. WE WANT THE CUP! This should be everyone's answer. Being greedy I want them to win 2 cups, so we have more than Pittsburgh. We have a great young nucleus at forward which we will hopefully keep together. Especially Giroux, Couturier, Schenn, Simmonds & Voracek. They are already fun to watch. Our D is ageing, but there are still players to be excited about. Goaltending is a generational problem but we've thrown $51m at it. Bryzgalov has had good games, but more bad games. Hopefully he will find his game. It would be nice not to be concerned about the position. I'd love to see Lindros' number retired.

Ray Skeates
Basingstoke, England
Philadelphia Flyers

The Philadelphia Flyers have an exciting future. To win a Stanley Cup in the near future is a goal every team wants to obtain, and I would like nothing more than to see the Flyers do so, but modelling the team after the Red Wings where they have qualified for the Playoffs for the last 21 seasons is a feat I would like to see in Philadelphia; building a solid core of young players who can compete season in, season out giving them a chance to win the Cup every year rather than a Cup win one year and fail to make the post-season for years after.

David Lidbury
Bristol, England
Philadelphia Flyers

The Cup. The team seems like they're always so close, but missing that vital piece. Find that missing piece and bring that silverware to Philly!!

Tim Barnes
Cambridge, England (born in New Jersey, USA)
Philadelphia Flyers

My hopes for the Coyotes? Simple! A stable ownership and a future in Arizona. The Coyotes, since their arrival in the desert, have always been fighting adversity but there is some light at the end of the tunnel. Throughout their history the Yotes have been regular attendees of the post season dance, but never progressing further than the first round, last year the Coyotes went one better and won their first ever playoff series. It was a season of firsts really, first hat-trick for Shane Doan, first Pacific Division title, first playoff series win and, with an end to the ownership saga in sight this could be a great summer for the Phoenix Coyotes. Getting consistent sell-outs have been difficult at the Jobing.com arena, but their are fans in the desert, the constant white-outs are proof of that! There are reasons to be optimistic in Phoenix, so lets have a howlin' good summer!

Mark Woodcock
Macclesfield, England
Phoenix Coyotes

Jonathan Northall

Obviously, my sole hope for the future right now is for the team to get a new owner. When and if that is settled my hope is for a postseason run that goes past the first round.

Emil Rutkowski
Uppsala, Sweden
Phoenix Coyotes

Another cup! Since 2009, the Pens just seem to have the worst playoff luck going, particularly the last two years. 2011 it was never going to happen without both Geno and Crosby and then 2012 was just the most bizarre series I have ever seen, I don't know whether it was down to the pressure of the expectation or the effect of too many starts in the year for Fleury.

James Bird
Burnley, England
Pittsburgh Penguins

My hopes for the future of the Pittsburgh Penguins are for the GM Ray Shero to make some more gutsy trades. The core has been together a long time now and maybe it's time for a change. The Penguins have a lot of trade bait that could potentially help them to receive two or three good players, for one of theirs. I would also like to see more young players continue to rise through the ranks from the AHL and like every hockey fan I'd love to see my team a realistic cup contender every year.

Tom Harding
Isle of Wight, England
Pittsburgh Penguins

My hope for the Pittsburgh Penguins is to turn back the clock to 2008. I want the Civic Arena rebuilt and Michel Therrien to be our head coach again. I am extremely superstitious when it comes to sports and I just knew that leaving the only home the Pens ever had, the Igloo, would bring bad karma on us. Sure enough the 'Guins have absolutely flopped in the playoffs each season in the new Consol Energy Center. There is no intimidation factor at the hygienic, bright CEC as there was at the rusty, cramped Civic/Mellon Arena. Visiting teams hated coming to Pittsburgh in the past, now they relish it. Part of this recent failure needs to be placed firmly on the shoulders of head coach Dan Bylsma though. Disco Dan, in my opinion, simply inherited Michel Therrien's talented team when the guys in black & gold stopped playing for him midway through the 2008-09 campaign. Energized by a young coach, himself only a couple of years removed as an active player, woke up the Pens and led them the Stanley Cup title...however, the Boys from The 'Burgh now seem complacent in the post season. Therrien would not put up with such laziness: he would have no problem benching star players for not performing up to expectations and never minced his words about the Pens problems to the media. Bylsma seems like a robot in comparison: he never makes ANY changes to the Pens playing style (even when it's not working as seen in last year's playoffs versus Philadelphia) and never criticizes any of the players in interviews.

Robert Campbell
Pittsburgh, USA (now Uppsala, Sweden)
Pittsburgh Penguins

As a Pittsburgh Penguins fan, I have already been through the mill somewhat over the past 12 years or so. But now we have a new home and a stable future I'm now looking at other areas. In the medium term, and whilst no team has a right to win a Stanley Cup, I would love this current group to fulfil its potential and go on to win another one. But I fear that the cap ceiling and the younger player's growing salary demands will result in the break up of the group before they can win another. Longer term, I appreciate having seen some pretty lean times as a Pens fan that hockey is cyclical and that this current good run will likely not last indefinitely. So I what I'd simply like is for my team is to ride the inevitable lean periods out and build on the incredible foundations that Mario and his team have put down off the back of the 1990's cup wins and the legacy that Le Manifique has created so that the team is never forced to consider relocating again.

Rob Howe
Sheffield, England
Pittsburgh Penguins

Hope for the Leafs? Make the playoffs again and we'll take it from there. Seriously though, I do think the Leafs have stockpiled enough assets to make this team competitive. It has to address the biggest needs during this offseason but I do think we'll be seeing a more truculent and competitive hockey club from now on. As far as the Penguins go, I think the presence of key young cogs at key positions and depth down the middle makes the Pens a perennial contender for years to come and that's more of a fact than it is hope.

Jonathan Northall

Can't hope for anything better than that.

Mislav Jantoljak
Zagreb, Croatia
Pittsburgh Penguins / Toronto Maple Leafs

As a Sharks fan, that should be so obvious! WE WANT THE CUP IN SAN JOSE…I'd hate to think that Marleau and Thornton could retire without ever getting their hands on the Stanley Cup…When you see the passion that Sharks' fans in the Bay Area and worldwide have and how the team has grown to take its place alongside the more dominant U.S. sports scene franchises such as the world-famous San Francisco 49ers, then you realise what a journey they have been through. From the Cow Palace to the Shark Tank and the growth in hockey in California in schools and the often mentioned 'one of the loudest buildings in the NHL' on TV broadcasts, then you know this franchise deserves a cup!!! And so do I after all the time, money, energy, emotion and late nights I have invested…

Jason Dunn
Woking, England
San Jose Sharks

I hope that we can maintain this level of success and energy. This was our first year in the playoffs since 2009 and before that it was before the lockout. We've grown as a team in the style that Coach Hitchcock has given us and I think, as long as we can balance our contracts out, we could have a good team for a number of years to come!

Grant Sales
High Wycombe, England
St Louis Blues

The Lightning have a strong future ahead of them, with great ownership, hall of fame GM, a dynamic coach and a guy who just scored 60 goals in a season. With the right moves over the next couple of summers. Most important of all a true number one goaltender. I'd love our future to be a consistent contender for the holy grail of Lord Stanley's cup. As let's all be honest, he needs another tan.

Nathan Cartmel
Bristol, England (now Tampa, FL, USA)
Tampa Bay Lightning

Ice Hockey Nights in Europe

I can honestly say that I see bright future for the Lightning and am very optimistic. As long as the core, Vinik-Yzerman-Boucher, stays I'm confident we'll see the Lightning become a very dangerous and good team, with regular playoff appearance. I'm very excited for the upcoming season. As for the questions what I would like for the team – well it's been quite obvious that scoring/forwards aren't an issue for the Lightning. It's the goalie situation and most importantly the defence that needs to be improved – by a lot. I believe Yzerman will be able to acquire defensemen that will be up to the task. It will be also very interesting to see whether the Lightning get Luongo or not, and if they do at what price.

Katerina Brzonova
Zlin, Czech Republic
Tampa Bay Lightning

I think I'd like my team (The Maple Leafs) to finally get a new owner that cares about winning, someone who shares the same ethics that the late Conn Smythe had when he owned the team, the likes of a pension plan ownership and now a multimillion dollar joint media ownership there is no passion to win championships, sadly they just care about their wallets, we need that Conn Smythe owner back that will do whatever it takes to create a championship team, instil pride back into management and players alike, that attitude won the Leafs their cups, sadly without that type of ownership nothing else will be truly resolved. We have a good farm team with a great coach, we also have a coach on the Leafs that finally seems to know what he's doing, we need a GM that can build a competing team and add the small pieces we need to turn things around, we need that GM that's willing to give the farm players a try in the NHL without sending them down as soon as they've come up but yet showed their worth.

AJ
Not disclosed
Toronto Maple Leafs

I'm in a comfortable spot these days, cheering for a team that finished with 100+ points for four consecutive seasons. I may sound minimalist, but if it ain't broke, don't fix it - I just want my Vancouver Canucks to stay this way: always competitive, always in the contender group, kind of like Detroit Red Wings. It may sound harsh, but I think only adolescent fans can seriously believe a team "has to" win a Stanley Cup to be successful... why bother watching 82 games of the regular season then? As for me, I will wait patiently for our date with Lord Stanley and icing a perennial contender is a great way of helping the team to eventually reach that Holy Grail. This day will come, but the "this is the year!!!!" approach is a bit shallow. Goal scoring droughts, goalies' hot and cold streaks, short term injuries, long term injuries, playoff injuries, suspensions... Many, many factors. And there are always a few teams in a similar spot, with similar appetites and proper personnel. There is one hope for the future, one thing I want to see changed. As much as I like most of my Canucks, I'm also excited with following prospects and the draft. Canucks are very conservative when it comes to introducing youngsters to the big leagues.

Michał Pręgowski
Warsaw, Poland
Vancouver Canucks

I think the obvious answer is to win a Stanley Cup. Division titles, Presidents Cups or long unbeaten runs don't mean anything at the end of the year so I'd love to see the Caps win a Cup preferably while Ovechkin is still captain.

Hana Imiolczyk
Merthyr Tydfil, Wales
Washington Capitals

My hopes for the future of the Winnipeg Jets are nothing more nothing less than making the playoffs if not the next season then soon. Getting deep in the playoffs. I'd be perfectly happy with that. This team has never been in the second round, not even as the Atlanta Thrashers. I want them to feel the pressure of the playoffs, get used to it and make it so far that the Cup is getting into your head. I want them to earn respect in the NHL, not to be the team you should be able to beat, I want to see our young talents grow into first-class players. I want the MTS centre never to be quiet.

Štěpánka Černá
Dolní Němčí, Czech Republic
Winnipeg Jets

To finish, I'd like to share my wishes for all teams in the NHL. I hope that they can uncover far more fans like these that are featured in the book. What I'd like the reader to take away from this book is that it's not about making a case for special treatment just because of our location. For me, it's about showing that commitment to your team can manifest itself in many forms. For all hockey fans, wherever you may be, we all love the game. This book could easily be about fans in Australasia or any other continent. We may wear different colours, follow different teams but we are all one hockey nation.

APPENDIX 1 – LIST OF CONTRIBUTORS

Bulgaria

Ivelina Toteva   Gabrovo

Croatia

Mislav Jantoljak   Zagreb

Czech Republic

Michal Belšán   Chomutov

Štěpánka Černá   Dolní Němčí

Katerina Brzonova   Zlin

Denmark

Kristina Stryhn Laursen Copenhagen

England

Vicki Morgan   Basingstoke

Janne Virtanen   Basingstoke

Ray Skeates   Basingstoke

Andrew Saunders   Birmingham

Kelly Marriot   Bournemouth

Daruish Gorgirzadeh   Bournemouth

Andrew Best   Bracknell

Ice Hockey Nights in Europe

Allan Allison	Bristol
Andreas Tatt	Bristol
Gavin Clarke	Bristol
David Lidbury	Bristol
Nathan Cartmel	Bristol
James Bird	Burnley
Dan Birkin	Burton upon Trent
Amy Hill	Camberley
Tim Barnes	Cambridge
Richard Trowbridge	Cheltenham
Andy Macleod	Congleton
Stuart Coles	Coventry
Daniel Betts	Coventry
Daniel Hartley	Darwen
Melanie Warn	Devon
Bradley Marsh	Essex
Robert Weaver	Gloucestershire
Grant Sales	High Wycombe
Richard Hardy	Hinckley
Callum Sweeting	Hull
Dale Casson	Hull
Ollie Jenvey	Isle of Wight
Tom Harding	Isle of Wight

Jonathan Northall

Mark Rackham   Kent
Joanne Turner   Leeds
Stephen Butler   Leicester
Dave Stanley   Liverpool
Steve Robinson   London
Andy Parsons   London
Tom Mannington   London
Adam Phillips   Luton
Mark Woodcock   Macclesfield
Steve McCaskill   Maidstone
George Royle   Malmesbury
Gareth Dutton   Manchester
Rebecca Hindle   Manchester
Rebecca Hindle   Manchester
Gord Turner   Manchester
Pete Hagan   Manchester
Rachael Eardley   Manchester
Dean Colasurdo   Manchester
Nick Gresty   Manchester
Mike Fuller   Newcastle
Rob Carter   Newcastle
Katy Parles   Newcastle upon Tyne
Jamie Mash   Northallerton

Ice Hockey Nights in Europe

Nathan Hollis	Norwich
Adam Webster	Nottingham
Junaid Hussain	Nottingham
Phil Holding	Nottingham
Nigel Morris	Oldbury
Sandra Pascoe	Penzance
Daniel Daw	Plymouth
Matt Merritt	Portsmouth
Alan Giles	Reading
Alex Nunn	Romford
Tony Harrison	Rutland
Kimmi Noble	Sheffield
Rob Howe	Sheffield
Elliott Hall	Sheffield
Youri Banville	Shrivenham
Ed Johnston	Somerset
Rob Aherne	Stafford
Benn Mixer	Stalham
Chris Bluff	Stockton-On-Tees
Joe Alderson	Stoke-on-Trent
Matthew de Bohun	Suffolk
Andrew Bell	Sunderland
Joan Chisholm	Washington

Jonathan Northall

James Willis	Watford
Jason Dunn	Woking
Stuart Wilson	York

Finland

Petri Kalajainen	Not disclosed
Satu Vanhanen	Joensuu
Ville Lampinen	Vantaa

France

Natacha Laporte	Strasbourg

Germany

David Trippler	Mainz
Neumann Family	Schwäbisch Hall

Iceland

Orri Smarason	Reykjavík

Italy

Emanuela Pozzi	Cernusco sul Naviglio
Silvia Bertolini	Milan

Ice Hockey Nights in Europe

Latvia

Elina Lazdina	Talsi

Northern Ireland

Raymond Jackson	Ballymena

Jack (Aaron) Stoops	Bangor

Eilis Phillips	Belfast

Christopher Barr	Dungannon

Norway

Thomas Olsen	Oslo

Poland

Paweł Jachowski	Siedlce

Bartek Pexu	Warsaw

Mikołaj Wójcik	Warsaw

Krzysztof Sankiewicz	Warsaw

Michał Pręgowski	Warsaw

Republic of Ireland

Diarmuid Murray	Dublin

Jonathan Northall

Scotland

David Robertson	Aberdeen
Neil Ritchie	Aberdeen
Glenn Innes	Aberdeen
Matthew Milne	Edinburgh
Darren Morgan	Glasgow
Katrina Gordon	Glasgow
Ryan McCue	Glasgow
Sharon Wedley	North Ayrshire
Aimee Docherty	Port Glasgow
Iain McKay	St Andrews

Slovakia

David Púchovský	Bratislava
Michal Heely	Michalovce
Michal Hežely	Michalovce

Slovenia

Sanja Prošek	Ljubljana

Sweden

Mattias Boström	Stockholm
Dan Edlund	Stockholm

Ice Hockey Nights in Europe

Emil Rutkowski   Uppsala

Robert Campbell   Uppsala

Wales

Chris Roderick   Ammanford

Kenny Jones   Caernarfon

James Cartwright   Cardiff

Hana Imiolczyk   Merthyr Tydfil

APPENDIX 2 – USEFUL SITES

Team Links

http://twitter.com/British_Avs

http://twitter.com/BritPensFanClub

http://twitter.com/EuroCaps

http://twitter.com/Eurolanche

http://twitter.com/FlyersFansUK

http://twitter.com/NYRANGERUK

http://twitter.com/NYRGBR

http://twitter.com/Oilers_UK

http://twitter.com/UK_Devils_Fans

http://twitter.com/uk_isles

http://twitter.com/UKBRUINS

http://twitter.com/UKCoyotes

http://twitter.com/UKNYRangers

http://twitter.com/UKVanFan

http://twitter.com/WpgJetsUK

General Sites

http://icenationuk.com/

http://ontheflyhockey.com/category/nhl-2/

http://uknhl.wordpress.com/

http://www.ukamericansportsfans.com/category/nhl

Printed in Great Britain
by Amazon.co.uk, Ltd.,
Marston Gate.